LEAN STONE PUBLISHING

"Turn the Page And Live a Better Life"

www.leanstonebookclub.com

indirect, which are incurred as a result of the use of information contained within this document, including, but not limited to,
 —errors, omissions, or inaccuracies.

Etiquette, Bundle I

Etiquette, How to Be a Gentleman

Table of Contents

Etiquette

A Guide to the Most Common Etiquette Rules and Social Situations where Etiquette Matters

Introduction

PROBABLY THE BEST BOOK CLUB ONLINE...

"If you love books. You will <u>love</u> the Lean Stone Book Club"

*** <u>Exclusive Deals</u> That <u>Any</u> Book Fan Would <u>Love</u>! ***

Visit leanstonebookclub.com/join

(IT'S FREE)!

To begin with, I would like to both thank you and congratulate you for downloading the book, "Etiquette – A Guide to the Most Common Etiquette Rules and Social Situations where Etiquette Matters!"

The term 'Etiquette' has generally been known to imply British Elizabethan Era starched white collars and feminine curtsies, at least that is what the common man seems to understand from the term. Empirically speaking however, etiquette is far from a lost art from across the pond, it is more casually referred to as manners in most current conversations, and yet the essence of the term remains the same.

Both terms refer to the socially acceptable 'norms' dictated to govern human behavior in certain social situations. Unfortunately since these sets of rule are something of an unwritten constitution, it is easy for it to become difficult to understand or even accurately emulate for outsiders. Which is why we bring to you this guide to common etiquette rules as they pertain to most modern social situations.

Now this may seem like a lot of information to process, so allow us to make this easier for you. The book you hold contains, in addition to a brief history of etiquette, the social etiquette outlines for nine specific scenarios, and each segmented into its own chapter.

We start with the history to give you a sense of why etiquette is necessary, and then go on to discuss the individual scenarios. One of the first chapters covers etiquette at the dinner table in a household, simple manners you can teach your children and that you should practice yourself for small casual dinners. We then deal with restaurant manners and tipping, both slightly more complex situations, but a great stepping stone for slightly larger social events such as parties, weddings, funerals all of which are later addressed in separate chapters.

Another thing most people forget is that etiquette is not limited to social interactions, there are guidelines that govern how one is supposed to dress, behave at interviews, workplaces, and even while travelling abroad. In fact in the advent of online social media has even created a certain outline of acceptable behavior or rather etiquette for online interactions as well as real-life social interactions, all of which is addressed in the book at hand.

For now, thanks again for downloading this book, I hope you enjoy it!

Chapter 1 - Etiquette: Social Norms and Why We Need Them

"The rules of good manners are the traffic lights of human interaction."

– Professor. Pier Forni, John Hopkins University

Mankind by definition is a social being. Like most other sentient beings we too crave social interaction and in many ways require it to live a happy and fulfilled life. The problem that often arises, especially in this growing era of globalization, is that while people are freely mixing, using a common language to interact, we often fail to realize that there needs to be common social rules as well, to better shepherd these masses of inter-mixed cultures easily without causing offence.

In fact, for most people not knowing certain specific social norms has on occasion lead to a tendency to be excluded from social events. Have you ever had that moment when you said something, and saw absolutely nothing wrong with what you said, but all on a sudden everyone in the room was looking at you with appalled shock – and all you could think was - 'What did I say?'

That was you making a social faux pas.

Remember, there is more to good manners than sipping your tea the right way. These specific sets of rules allow us to identify with each other and find common ground. They also allow us to ensure that we don't infringe on anyone else's space even though we may not think we are doing so.

Etiquette is as such, a social vaccine of sorts, one that helps prevent the negative impact of ignorance on social connections. And while not many may deem this to be important, the truth of the matter is it is very important.

Why?

Well, because while some may find this ignorance endearing or forgivable, there are many others who will judge you and not only find you lacking, but unfit for their social circle.

It is importance because it allows you to now compete with equal footing, and because you are human and therefore in order to interact with other humans you need to conform to a certain level.

It is important - because once you are done with all your rebelling and your posturing you will realize that there are norms or rules of conduct even amongst rebels. Etiquette is not something you can escape, so instead of looking at it as a ball and chain, think of it as a weapon that, with a little practice, you can wield with remarkable results!

So let's get started shall we?

Chapter 2 – The Trifecta of Table Manners

While there are admittedly way more than just three rules when it comes to table etiquette, the many rules of dining at a table can in fact be sectioned under three main heads, which is how we will be discussing them. These three areas deal with, table settings, table manners themselves in terms of dining, and dining table conversations.

We will be discussing each of the heads in depth, with a noteworthy focus on the most basic rules and then a more cursory glance at the more ceremoniously observed formalities. With all of the rules being discussed under specific heads and sub-headings, you will have a better opportunity to be able to pick up on how each of the norms relate to each other as well as, an understanding of which circumstances they would be required in, as opposed to which circumstances they could be held a little more loosely in.

Simple enough?

Great!

Let's dig in!

Table Settings

Let's say you are about to host a small dinner party, for a few office colleagues and your boss or your in-law's and the woman of your dreams – either way you desperately need to get this right. Because like it or not you are about to be judged, on every aspect of your hosting skills, and since it's most likely a dinner party – the first place you are most likely to screw up is when it comes to setting the table.

Now, keep in mind that table settings involve a number of things including, the actual seating, the place settings, the utensils, the dinnerware, and even the glassware!

If you are holding a relatively casual party, your main concern while setting the table should be the placement of the dinnerware and utensils. The general rules that the utensils need to be on level with the bottom line of the dinnerware while the dinnerware itself should be approximately one inch from the edge of the table.

The utensils need to be in clear view, and yet not too far away from the plates, so once again approximately one inch, from the plate, while you will need about fifteen inches between that and your next place setting. Your glassware needs to be placed approximately an inch above the tip of the dinner knife.

An easy tip to remember is that the utensils and glassware are placed based on the courses. Generally the one's that will be used first are placed in closest proximity. Another hostess tip is to hold the utensils at the midpoint between the tip and end to avoid smudges or fingerprints.

Table Manners

Now that you have your table all set and are ready for your dinner guests – the next question is about behavior. How are you expected to behave, what are you expected to do and what are you expected not to do.

Well, most table manners are so basic they have most probably been ingrained in you from childhood. For instance when it comes to eating your food, chewing with your mouth closed, not making noise while you eat etc. yet there are still some rules that are equally important if not as widely known. When it comes to eating for instance, it is important that the diner wait for their host or hostess to start before they touch their food. It is equally important to wait and finish chewing and swallowing their food before they have a sip of water or any other beverage. It is also considered polite to only cut into one

particular food item at a time, mixing your food in your plate
is considered highly uncouth and absolutely unacceptable at
most dinner tables.

Other than actual eating, there are other rules as well, for
instance not only is it important to keep your elbows off the
table, but it is also considered impolite not to be sitting up
straight. Once you are seated you should immediately reach
for the napkin and place it on your lap. This napkin should be
left unfolded towards the left-hand side of the place setting
when you remove yourself from the table. Once you have
finished eating, your utensils are meant to be left face up, and
together on your plate, not on the side or crossed.

Table Conversation

The third most important thing at a dinner table is
conversation. Conversation at the dinner table should be light
and entertaining, it is also important to be inclusive, so don't
bring up topics that leave out a specific guest – it is both rude
and insulting.

 Regardless of where you are seated, your obligation as it
pertains to conversation generally extends to the person across
from you, and the two people on either side of you. In smaller
dinner parties with four or six people, it is generally expected
that your conversation will include all the other people from
the table as well but in larger parties, your immediate circle
will suffice.

When it comes to conversation topics, it is important to ask
open-ended questions on appropriate topics. Recent trips, new
life events such as becoming a new parent or being recently
married are also a great conversation starter. If you are not
that familiar with the person you have been seated with, it is
acceptable to break the ice by talking about your hosts and
how you know them – this allows you to exchange information
and learn new stories.

Remember there is etiquette to govern the way you behave in these conversations as well. If you are the one engaging the other person, it is important to maintain a tone that is moderate and yet jovial. Avoid any overt displays of emotion and try to ensure you are not boring the other person. Furthermore as a listener you need to not only pay attention to your conversation partner but also participate without interrupting for example – 'That's fascinating! Tell me more.' This helps show you are equally engaged in the conversation and helps project a positive vibe at the table.

While these are just some of the many basic table etiquettes that govern our modern world they are enough for you to get by with just a little bit of practice!

Chapter 3 – The Restaurant Rulebook

While most of the basic table manners when it comes to eating out at a restaurant are the same as those you would display at home, there are quite a few significant differences as well. For instance when it comes to eating out there are three main stages, you have the planning stage, the arrival stage and finally the billing. The most important restaurant manners will be elaborated on below based on these three points of reference.

The Planning Stage

To start with let's talk about how the outing is planned.

Since a restaurant outing is at a foreign venue, the rule of thumb is to always ensure that your guests have been provided with an easy location, an idea about the dress code and adequate time to reach the venue. It is your job to ensure the venue is booked. The last thing you want is for your guests to reach the restaurant and be waiting to be seated.

Also booking early allows you to select a specific area to be seated in, such as a quiet corner or a window view. When deciding on a venue, try to incorporate your guests preferences and ensure you are not taking them to a place they won't be able to eat, for example if they are vegan or prefer kosher food, check ahead and ensure that the restaurant serves what you need or pick another venue.

If you are open to it, you could also think about presenting your guests with a list of two to three restaurants and allowing them to select, to suit their preference. If not just ensure that you have chosen a restaurant that caters to a wider selection so that everyone will most likely have something to suit his or her tastes. It is also usually a good idea to pick a place you have been to before, that way you are not only aware of the expense, and service but also will most likely be more comfortable when you ask for the bill and are tipping.

It is equally important that you arrive before your guest so that you are there to welcome them, a smart thing to do is to call ahead at the restaurant, reconfirm the reservation and wait to receive your guests at the bar or table.

The Arrival Stage

The number one rule of 'arrival' etiquette is to make sure you are never ever late! Especially if you are the host – in fact, if you are the host the best thing you can do is arrive early and wait for your guests. This not only gives you time to check on the table and input and specific preferences for the wine or billing method but it also give you time to settle in and not look as harried.

When you arrive at a restaurant however, your etiquette does not merely extend to your guests. As soon as you arrive, you will generally be greeted by a valet and it is customary to both greet your valet and to remember to tip them on your way out. The same goes for when you are greeting your Maitre d', be polite and say 'hello' before you begin to speak to them about your seating preferences.

Another thing to keep in mind when entering a restaurant, both as a guest and as a host is that you don't want to clutter your table with packages, or coats – instead remember to check in your coat, as well as any packages or briefcases you may be carrying. While women are known to take their purses to the table, it is important to never place the purse on the actual table and instead try to place it near her feet or on her lap.

Your next concern is seating. If you have arrived alone, then you are expected to wait for at least one other person before you ask to be seated, however if there are two or more of you, you are expected to be seated while you wait for the rest of your party. If you are not satisfied with your table it is best to calmly ask for an alternative table, if you had a table booked and it was not held you are within your rights to leave and find a better restaurant. Since much of Victorian etiquette has trickled down into modern day etiquette, it is important to allow women preferential seating and then seat the males. Guests of honor are generally privy to similar preferential seating.

The Billing Stage

The final stage of restaurant dining is the simplest and yet the most sensitive. Money matters are generally held to be indelicate, so if you are the host and are paying the bill it is best if you could arrange to pay before the event or discreetly at the table. Whatever you do, ensure that you don't have any squabbling over the bill at the table it is both impolite and very crass.

If it is a joint bill, ensure that, the server is notified before you ask for the bill so that they can bring separate checks, instead of you having to turn your dinner table into a impromptu math class.

Another issue you should keep in mind when you are considering paying the bill is tipping. Generally restaurant protocol dictates that you tip your server twenty percent of your total bill, however if there have been any upsets at the table, you may want to tip them a bit more.

Keep in mind that the restaurant experience is about more than a simple meal, it is about engaging your guests in a suitable environment with agreeable patronage of a restaurant that allows you to showcase your ability to both mingle with them and to appropriately interact with your servers.

Chapter 4 - Putting the 'P' in Party Protocol

While family dinner and restaurant dates may be difficult waters to navigate, the real trouble starts to hit when you have all of society watching your every move, we are talking of course about those glittery social events that tend to pop up on your social calendar ever so often. Now, while these glittery social parties may not be a day-to-day staple for you, they are without a doubt the single most embarrassing place to make a social mistake. In fact, the reason they are so rife with possible mess up's is because they are equally rife with possibilities.

Which is exactly why in this chapter we are about to not only outline the socially acceptable behavior that is expected of you at these events but also what you need to avoid to make the most out of these opportunities. Like our earlier chapters we are going to split the nuances of party etiquette into three major heads and then elaborate on the major points within those heads that are going to be relevant to you.

Pre-Party Panache

Before you even set foot in your little society glitterama you are going to brush up on all of you social know how especially if you want to make the most of the event. Let's start by talking about what you are going to need to do - beforehand to make sure you are maintaining party protocol.

When you are invited to elaborate parties like this it is important to make sure you respond to the invitations with a clear definitive answer. A non-committal answer is not only frustrating; it is impolite since you host is now unsure whether or not to save a plate for you. Furthermore, since events like these are generally seated events a last minute addition or a last minute dropout forces your host to take on a massive headache for seating, dinner and even planned events. So whatever you do, make sure that you have properly, and clearly provided an answer and do so as early as you can so that your hosts know what to plan for.

The next pre-party prep is of course to buy a present! Now, you don't have to go off and buy some elaborate gift that breaks the bank but do buy something that is a nice thank you for your meal, and the general rule is to usually spend something in that price bracket. Flowers are best if sent in early with a hand-written note, but if you want to bring the gift yourself try a bottle of wine, or even just a nice box of chocolates.

And the last, pre-party rule is quite simple – don't be early. While being late is a marginally less attractive alternative, it is by far the one that will be preferred by your hosts, especially because of how much of a hassle you are going to be if you show up while they are still preparing. Don't do it. If you absolutely must – be late, but do not under any circumstances be early.

Social Mingling

Now, every host's worst nightmare is the aloof guest. Yes, you know the one I'm talking about, the socially awkward guest standing in a corner nursing a glass of wine accidentally spilling it on everyone who tries to speak to them and thereby creating all sorts of unwanted mayhem.

If this is you, you can rest assured that this is your last invite.

If it isn't – this is how you can ensure you don't become that person.

The first trick of the trade is to smile. A smile will go a long way and believe it or not can be a great conversation starter. The next trick is to be a good listener, if your host is talking or one of their guests are, be an engaged audience, slowly but surely enough this will get you into a few conversations and it will also help you host, since they don't have to be a part of that lengthy lecture and can move around and mingle themselves.

Another bone of contentions is the phone dilemma. In modern day society, taking your phone or tab out in the middle of a social party is the height of disrespect. It is the Victorian equivalent of snapping a fan in front of your face and looking elsewhere – not only rude but a clear slight against your hosts.

Party Post-Partum's

Now, just because you have made it through the maze of social expectations that have governed the party and the events leading up to it, does not mean you are home free just yet. In fact, you simply have two things left to do.

Number one is to leave. Believe it or not the only thing worse than a guest that shows up early is a guest who stays late and doesn't know when it is time to go. If you aren't sure just keep an eye out for the rest of the guests and follow the herd, if you see that it's getting late, or that your hosts are getting cranky, find a polite way to excuse yourself and leave.

The second thing in the list is to make sure you send a thank-you note. Now, a lot of people think that it's acceptable to send an email or a text because it's efficient. It's not. Your hosts went to the trouble of inviting you to their home and provided you with a seat at their table – the least you can do is pen them a thank-you note.

All in all, social norms as they pertain to social events are pretty straightforward. For the most part they merely build on the dinner and restaurant rules, and add in a few boundaries about what you are supposed to be doing while you are already adhering to those rules.

Chapter 5 - Of Church Bells and Mourning Veils

Another two social etiquette areas that are massively complex are weddings and funerals. Not only are these two particular events difficult to navigate, but also because of their nature, they are most definitely not somewhere you want to be applying a trial and error test trial.

Not to worry, spouses to be and family or friends of the bereaved, this chapter will walk you through everything you need to know about wedding announcements, ceremony do's and don'ts, and even where to discreetly list your registry! It also covers funeral social niceties, outfits, and honorariums. Think of it as you're a to z manual on all major church events.

What You Need to Know About Your Wedding Bells

Let's start off on happy note and talk weddings first. In today's world of hash-tags and Facebook status updates it's hard to keep track of the actual traditions that weddings generally entail. It is harder still to update these old traditions and find a way to still stay current. In this chapter we help you deal with all of these necessary updates, as well as the more basic rules, such as who to invite, how to send out invites, where to register and many other wedding related norms.

First off, let's talk about the announcement. An engagement is a big deal, especially for close friends and family – which is precisely why, no matter how excited you are or how ecstatic you cannot simply upload a picture and update your status, until you have at the very least informed your parents and close relatives. After you've done so the best thing to do is have a discussion with your partner and come to a mutual decision as to whether or not you would like to make a change on social media.

Next up let's talk about the invitations. Generally the best option is to go with printed or handwritten invitations, this allows the couple to provide a bit of a personal touch, just make sure your invitation is just about the wedding and doesn't include wedding registry information on the card itself. The most common trend currently is to add a separate note about the wedding registry in the envelope, but not directly on the card. Furthermore if your invitations are RSVP's as the probably are the best thing to do is give the guests about two weeks to figure out logistics and then start making follow-up calls to determine your final guest list. Speaking of which, also keep in mind that who you are inviting is just as if not more important than the invitations themselves so do remember to always invite family first and then close friends. Colleagues are not a necessity, but if you do want to invite them remember to do so personally and not in a public or office setting so that other co-workers aren't offended. Also keep in mind that at the wedding itself it is important to greet each of these people individually, and not only is paying for an extra dozen of plates expensive, faking a smile any longer than you have to is arduous. So only invite the people you really want to be there.

Funeral Fundamentals

Funerals are even more sensitive than weddings, they are the one place where it is vital that you not cause any embarrassments, by being accidentally clumsy or ignorant. Nevertheless, funeral etiquette rules are much more relaxed today then they were in previous eras so it is mostly just to do with what you wear and your interactions at the funeral.

To start, it is important, to wear something clean and respectful. There are occasions when having been caught off guard, with a death in the family, one feels that they don't have the 'right' outfit, the rule of thumb is to simply go for a black suit if you are a man, nothing flashy, and a black dress, or failing that a dress in an equally dark color, such as dark blue or plum.

Once you have reached the service, you are expected to be greeting the many people who have already arrived. Admittedly, while this is not going to be something you enjoy doing, especially while people come up and repeatedly offer you condolences, it is important for you to remember that this is not about you. These people are here to pay their respects to a person they cared about and it is your duty to allow them to do so.

Yes, many of these condolences are going to be inappropriate or awkward, not intentionally, but usually because some people simply don't know what to say, and more importantly what not to say. If you believe it is all getting too much for you, excuse yourself and retire to your seat. As a family member, your seat is usually in one of the first two pews of the church, away from the rest of the guests so if you feel like you need a break from them you can easily slip up to your seat and focus on the prayers for a while.

After the funeral, it is important that you pay honorariums to the clergy and singers before you have left. It is not exactly billed, but it is generally held to be customary. Similarly, once you have gone home and cleared your head a bit you should also pen down thank –you notes, at the very least, to those involved actively in the service, but many people send thank you notes to everyone who came. – It is really just a matter of preference.

Just remember, in both of these events you are part of the main party, and your social duty extends mostly to your guests as well as yourself which is why it is so important to fixate on the proper etiquette expected at the ceremonies.

Chapter 6 - The Clothes Maketh the Man!

One of the most difficult areas of social etiquette, especially for novices is the proper understanding of dress codes or the social etiquette behind proper outfits for specific occasions. Now, while special occasions in modern times have a much narrower scope than what was the norm back in eighteenth century Britain, the need of a constructive code of attire for specific occasions does linger.

For specific private events such as dinner parties, or dates dress codes vary vastly from what would be considered acceptable at a more casual setting such as a picnic or casual get together. Either way it is important that one understand what one is expected to be wearing and what they are expected not to wear, not just because they need to conform to such dress codes often times for entering specific areas but also because failure to do so is often seen as odd at the least and inexcusably rude at the worst.

To make this simpler we are going to explore traditional constructs of what entails appropriate dressing as it pertains to men and women in formal, semi-formal and casual settings.

Women's Attire

A person's attire is the equivalent of the cover of a book. It is regardless of any clichéd proverbs exactly what they will be judged by. It is a fact of life that women traditionally tend to face dressing dilemma's a bit more often than men, which is why we will start by discussing what is appropriate formal attire, what is acceptable semi-formal attire and what constitutes casual attire for women in today's world.

Now, when it comes to formal wear, most women see this as an exciting break from the norm and feel an urge to go all out. Please don't. As interesting as a formal event invite must be, you still need to focus on what you can wear to the event based

on the event itself. If the event is a more restrained
conventional event, it is best to go ahead with an evening dress
of a modest length. Floor length dresses are your safest option,
since there is little that can go wrong there. However if the
invitation specifically says the dress code is cocktail you can
perhaps be a bit more experimental and go with mid-calf
embellish dresses or better yet an elaborate ball gown.

Semi-Casual wear for women, in contrast usually still does
mean a dress, just a less formal one, like perhaps a sundress of
a long maxi-gown. Pairing either with a smart blazer can amp
up the dress easily, and in fact also goes well with dress pants
and a short-collared shirt. Jeans, mini-skirts, shorts and
basically all other forms of feminine garments are acceptable
as casual wear, although it is important that, much like in
formal events the outfit chosen is appropriate for the outing in
question.

Dress codes for women, however are not limited to outfits.
Instead, it is important to ensure that the makeup, and
accessories are also perfectly in sync with the outfit. If you are
wearing a casual outfit, it is best to avoid heavy makeup or
sky-high heels, instead opt for a fresh faced natural look and
sandals or slippers.

Boots are also a great alternative.

In contrast when you are dealing with evening wear, it is
important that the makeup and accessories both complement
the dress, and since it's an evening program you can generally
get away with using darker, or richer colors in your makeup –
footwear is generally heels, or shoes, closed ballet flats are also
considered acceptable in some situations, for instance if you
are pregnant, elderly etc.

Men's Attire

Oddly enough, despite its deceptively simplistic outlook,
formal attire for men is a much more complex area, which of
course leads to hours of mulling over clothing swatches, the

correct lapel style, matching trouser braiding and of course the tie. Casual and Semi-Formal outfits are slightly less of a conundrum, but still need to be examined.

But let us start with formal wear. For men, formal wear, true formal wear is generally limited to very few officious occasions, mostly they tend to simply opt for a semi-formal jacket and dress pants. For these handful of occasions where they are expected to dress up however, the rule of thumb is to go with black. Not only are black suit standard but they fit into almost any occasion, be it a funeral or a wedding. Also black has the added advantage of never going out of fashion.

A properly fitted dinner jacket is an investment. Not only can you wear it almost anywhere, but also its superior fit and cut will also make you seem a cut above the common rented crowd. Pair your dinner jacket with plain hemmed bottoms, and a shirt with turn down collar and you can't go wrong.

When it comes to semi-formal outfits, most men tend to prefer chord of chambrays with a formal shirt, possibly a short collar and often with sleeves turned up. Casual dressing is again very event specific, and can range anywhere from beach shorts to a pair of sturdy heavy-duty jeans. The trick to semi-formal and casual dressing is to make sure your outfit is tidy even if it isn't formal, casual button downs are always a classy option, but even a polo-shirt or a cotton tee can work as long as you look presentable. Remember to try to err on the side of caution and not wear anything inflammatory, you aren't a teenager at a concert anymore!

Ultimately, dress codes are an area of social etiquette that is precariously balanced on a set of continuously changing variables, so you will have to use your own judgment to a large extent, but these basic guidelines should help you figure out most of stakes.

Chapter 7 - The Six Secret Office Rules

Off all social situations the one's that require the most delicate handling, are those that are 'professional' social situations. It is only too easy to find yourself confused and unaware of the expected behavior during specific situations or even simply of the specific etiquette rules that are silently observed in office culture, without being explicitly stated. Because many of these rules differ from what is considered okay in social situations even in the more relaxed office conditions, it becomes difficult to identify the distinct boundaries that need to be respected in order for the proper observation of workplace etiquette.

Furthermore, these rules and regulations are what help your co-workers and superiors to vet you. Many companies place great value in employees who properly observe these regulations, not just because it's what the company expects, but also because it is exactly the kind of behavior they feel comfortable promoting in executives they wish to earmark for promotions or more public positions. This chapter will explore office etiquette, with an emphasis on appropriate attire, office kitchen rules, greetings, communication, workspace boundaries and international business norms.

Basic Office Attire

We've already spent some time discussing appropriate dress codes in the previous chapter, so it isn't necessary to go too in depth in the issue of proper office attire, but since we are giving the issue a cursory glance let us focus on what is generally held to be appropriate.

For office environments, women are generally expected to dress in office skirts alternatively pencil skirts, and tops. There are exceptions where wears dress pants may be acceptable, but for the most part pencil skirts, or some similar variation are held to be the best option. Friday's are generally more lax and it is acceptable to wear a dress or slightly less formal outfit – something that fits into the common definition of semi-formal should do well.

For men, the standard office attire is always a suit, with the semi-formal variation of chambrays and button down shirts being more appropriate for Friday's and out of office excursions.

Office Kitchen Rules

Office etiquette also extends to the proper and conscientious use of the common office kitchen. When using the office kitchen, it is important to remind yourself that this is a common kitchen shared by many other employees and is likely only cleaned one a day – the bottom line of which is that it is if you are using office kitchen supplies, you are customarily obligated to pick up after yourself, and keep the kitchen neat and tidy so as to avoid any unwanted infestations or even simply to avoid any messes.

Furthermore, it is also important to remember that this is not your home; it is not okay to 'borrow' someone else, soda or lunch under any circumstance.

Common treats left out for colleagues may be sampled, but it is important that you not over indulge and stick to just one portion. Another important rule is to ensure that you have not left behind an empty coffee pot, if you have in fact poured yourself the last cup of coffee at least brew a new pot before you take off with yours.

Greetings

A large part of office etiquette is based on the importance of carving out a positive image of yourself. One thing that helps to do so is to make sure that you are mindful of you behavior towards other office colleagues.

This can be as simple as greeting them with a 'hello' or 'good morning' and is best if catered too with additional courtesy 'thank you' when indicating appreciation. It is also considered important to ensure that you maintain eye contact and proper body posture while you do so.

Communication and Socializing

Office culture is largely constrained by specific social norms that dictate how one is expected to behave with other co-workers.

Some of the key rules you are going have to adhere to include adequately addressed phone responses, formal emails, and being respectful of other people's personal lives.

Alternative rules include, punctuality, avoiding conflict and most importantly hearing other people out instead of interrupting them, no matter what the situation may be. These little things go a long way in modifying your usual personality into one that is more office appropriate.

Workspace Boundaries

Another area of office etiquette that is unfortunately often overlooked is concerned with your office space and that of others.

When you are in an office you need to keep in mind that a person's office space is like their home, be it a cubicle or a corner office you need to treat it with equal respect, which is why you don't just barge into someone's cubicle, instead turn the corner and knock to let your colleague know you would like a word.

Also remember to keep your own space equally clean and tidy so that anyone who comes into your office is presented with a positive image of your personal space.

International Business Norms

With globalizations being what it is, more and more businesses are currently dealing with foreign clientele. As is expected foreign business cultures do on occasion vary from what is the usual North American standard. Which is why when dealing with such circumstances it is important to not only have an interpreter on board but also someone who can help explain cultural differences so that you may avoid giving offence.

All in all, business etiquette, be it in the workplace or in client meetings is something that needs to be diligently observed if you really want to create a positive impression at your office. Such essentials of business etiquette are your stepping stones as well as your areas of common ground, and should be treated with the care they obviously warrant.

Chapter 8 – The Seven Secret Rules about Travelling

While most of our etiquette series has focused on social interactions and situations, which are inductive to social interactions, there are a number of social etiquettes that govern the more silent forms of social communication as well. Generally, situations where you will be forced to display a clear hold on what is acceptable and what is not acceptable in terms of silent etiquette is mostly constrained to commutes or other travelling methods.

Since you tend to commute with all sorts of people, it is the one place where you are generally put into a complex colony of people, from all walks of life, and that is exactly why you find yourself faced with so many questions about 'travel manners'.

This particular chapter addresses the top ten rules that you will need to be observing while travelling or commuting if you are to maintain social etiquette, in an attempt to make adapting these rules into your own personal behavior.

Rule One: Lines are Single File

The absolutely most annoying thing that a person can do when you are attempting to board anything be it a bus, or train or plane, is attempt to cut in line. Seriously, stop. There are people who have been waiting patiently in line, if you weren't on time that is your problem that does not give you a right to attempt to barge in on someone else was.

Grow up! Also, while we are on the topic, don't make double lines and attempt to push through - that is as bad as double parking, if you wouldn't do that with your car what makes you think it's okay to do it in person?

Rule Two: Waiting to Board

This particular rule actually applies not just to boarding areas or bus stops, but also to reception areas or waiting rooms – in truth it should really just be common sense. If you are already seated, and notice other people who are in need of a seat, do not be so rude as to block adjacent seats with your luggage or knickknacks. It is rude, the very opposite of thoughtful and greedy.

Rule Three: Seating Etiquette

Another issue that comes up a lot is seating etiquette – the most common infringement on this particular front is the lack of forethought put into reclining seats. Yes, yes we get it's your seat and you want to take a nap or shut your eyes for a bit, but at the very least you could bend over and inform the person seated behind you that you are about to recline your seat so that they can ensure they aren't caught off guard, as the victim of a nasty juice spill or something equally preventable.

Rule Four: Turn Down the Volume

While you are on public transport, be it a plane or a bus, you are just one of many people on board, and while you may adore Metallica or Pink Floyd someone else may not share your enthusiasm or someone may be trying to put a tired baby to sleep either way, there is no reason they should have to be subject to you putting on your music on full blast.

This is why mankind created headphones. Use them. If you forgot yours at home, suffer in silence, or read a book. Just don't put your whims above the comfort of other paying passengers.

Rule Five: The Living-room syndrome

The Living-room syndrome is something we often see in long distance journey, generally it is used to cover a range of 'living-room' like behaviors displayed by passengers who are booked on a long flight or a long train ride, such behaviors include but are not limited to, taking off one's shoes, and propping your feet up, talking loudly on the phone all in all – the tendency to treat your surroundings like your living room.

The rule of thumb here is discretion. Long commutes are difficult, and sometimes your feet will start to ache from the high heels, or you will have to take a phone call, the trick is simply to do so in a manner that is discreet and one that does not adversely affect those around you.

Rule Six: Colleague Confidentiality

While most of travel etiquette centers on how to conduct yourself during a commute, another avenue of travel that needs specific deliberation, especially when it is of a business nature is the confidentiality of your travel companion. When you are going on a trip with someone you will most likely learn a lot about them, overheard phone calls, messages, arguments, conversations, all of it is likely to lead you to know a lot more about your colleague than you did when you left. The worst breach of etiquette would be to use that knowledge as a topic of gossip. Learn to keep the conversations you have had or overheard private; I'm sure you would expect the same of someone else.

Rule Seven: Tokens of Appreciation

If you have been on a recent trip, of any sort and especially if you have been to a foreign country, or even a domestic location based on an invite, the first thing you should have done as soon as you decided to go was pick up a token gift for your hosts. This applies not only to personal or social occasions but also to business trips – before you leave it is customary to thank your hosts, or host organizations and leave them a gift as a token of your appreciation.

As simple as these travel rules may seem, do keep in mind that these are general rules applicable to most places, however if you are travelling in a foreign country it is a good idea to read up on the cultures and customs of that country , especially since cultural norms tend to vary.

Chapter 9 - A Peek into the Do's and Don'ts of Dating Etiquette

Dating is something you have most likely been doing since you were fifteen years old, with all that wealth of experience behind you , I'll bet it's never really occurred to you that there could be things on a date that you have been doing wrong. Think about it, haven't you ever had a promising date, only to suddenly be cold-shouldered? Odds are the sudden mood change is probably because of some dating 'don't' that you decidedly did 'do'.

There is a lot about dating that can't be catalogued and organized, but the basic structure of behavior that is followed is somewhat of a common phenomenon. And while this basic structure is often modified to help adapt with modern takes on dating, it still provides a solid basis for acceptable and expected behavior.

Money Matters

One particular aspect of dating that is generally pretty complicated in first dates and normal relationship outings alike is the financial end of the date. Who pays? Who is expected to pay? When should you offer to pay? All of these questions however are largely circumstantial.

If it is a first date, protocol dictates that it generally expected that the male be the one to pick up the check, if you are a same sex couple, usually the male-dominant or the person who asks the other out is expected to pick up the bill. This is in no way written in stone however and a good date will always offer to split the bill or at least pick the tab up for some other part of the date. Remember ladies, it's not all on the man, and dating protocol extends to you as well – so if you are out on a first date, offer to pull your own weight.

In long-term relationships, money matters are generally understood, however if you feel like you have been bearing too much of the financial burden make a point to have a open conversation about it so that you can work out the problem. Suggest sharing the bill or alternatively taking turns when it comes to paying the bill.

Honesty is the Best Policy

Another important rule that most people expect to be adhered to when it comes to dating, is that the date will be honest with them. It is not just deceitful, but the height of impropriety. Many people seem to think it is okay to fudge the lines and think that lying about their professional or personal life is acceptable behavior.

They could not be more wrong. Lying to get a person into bed with you, or to get a person to keep seeing you is a horrendous appropriation of their affection, and one of the most inconsiderate moves a person can make, especially if it pertains to your relationship status, or profession. Instead be honest and upfront, people may surprise you and besides it is the right thing to do.

Meal-time Manners

Say you are out on a date, and the second your date realizes you are footing the bill, she decides to order the most expensive thing on the menu. What would you think? I'm guessing, that at the very least you are going to be massively under-impressed by her gold-digging tendency. Probability of you asking her out again also probably plummeted. You see manners matter even when it comes to the ordering of food on a date.

In fact, another important thing to avoid is drinking too much. Not only do multiple drinks add up to a much higher bill, but the more you drink the more you tend to start behaving inappropriately, an inability to hold your drink or to control how much you are drinking are the last things you want to be putting on display on your date.

Chomping on the Conversation:

The last thing we are going to be discussing on our dating protocol list is conversation topics. Now it is hard enough to try to figure out what you can and can't say on a date, but it can be harder still when it is a first date. The powers that be say that the smartest way you deal with conversation topics is by allowing yourself to stick to the positives. Talk about good things in your life and avoid topics like, bad breakups or sob stories of any kind until you are further into the dating cycle.

Also while you are having conversations always try to be attentive and interested. Not only does it go a long way in the projection of you being a good listener, it can also help ensure that you are learning more about your date.

And there you go, we have just outlined for you the major areas of social etiquette, that you should be paying careful attention to in the circumstance they may present themselves in. The importance of decorum should never be underestimated, and while you may have a sense of it now, I believe once you start actively applying these rules in your own personal life, the actual perks associated with appropriate etiquette will be a very pleasant surprise!

Conclusion

Society has a tendency to be made up of deep waters, which are in effect very difficult to navigate. Hopefully this book can help you with that, intended to act as a guide and compass for the novice traveler on these uncharted waters, **"Etiquette – A Guide to the Most Common Etiquette Rules and Social Situations where Etiquette Matters!"** is dedicated to helping you figure out everything about how to deal with social situations with aplomb, and minus the embarrassing stories.

These steps and stages that we have discussed in the book are all here to help you, teach you how to grow in these professional and personal settings so that not only is your image protected but it is also benefited from all the knowledge you have now acquired.

Finally, this book is a mere guide that can teach you to navigate the waters, but if you really want to be properly ordained you are going to have to practice these manners all the time on a daily basis until they become second nature to you and part of your lifestyle.

Properly executed manners not only make those around you more comfortable, but they help you fit seamlessly into any situation on, and therefore making you more successful person in the long run. Furthermore, on a more personal note, if you enjoyed this book, and have benefited from it, please take the time to share your thoughts and post a review on Amazon. It'd be greatly appreciated!

Thank you and good luck!

How to Be a Gentleman

What Every Modern Man Needs to Know about Manners and Behaviors to Attract Women

Introduction

First, I would like to thank you for buying the book "How to be a Gentleman – What Every Modern Man Needs to Know about Manners and Behaviors to Attract Women".

As you made the decision of downloading this book, this means you recognize that being a gentleman is a wise choice. This book addresses the issue of chivalry and why it is possibly the single, most attractive character trait a man should present. Plus, it outlines that being a gentleman is more than a adopting a style of conduct, but it is rather about altering your way of thinking and living.

As far as styles of conduct go, it's important to note that there is a world of difference between being a true gentleman and being merely nice in a given situation, as well as being an all-around nice guy in general. The way that the dictionaries have it, being nice simply implies the quality of being good-natured and/or kind. As you progress through the contents of this book, you will find that this personal trait is but a small fraction of all that which makes a gentleman. Furthermore, you are likely aware of the stigma associated with nice guys nowadays. More precisely, it concerns how nice guys often get the bad end of the bargain in many endeavors and interactions in life.

Unfortunately, this is often true indeed. As opposed to a man who is merely a nice guy, a gentleman does not get trampled over and stepped on just because he won't stand up for himself. On the contrary, a real gentleman holds his own and knows when to show strength of character and decisiveness with the aim of self-preservation, while still maintaining his chivalry and honor intact. A gentleman knows his own worth very well and has enough confidence not to get taken advantage of.

In this context, it is also interesting to consider the very origin of the word "nice." Namely, you may be surprised to learn that the word had a much different meaning in Middle English, in the period between the 12th and 15th century, where it was used to denote a person as being "stupid." The similar meaning holds true when you explore further into the past, where you'll find it meant anything from "ignorant" to "reserved."

Regardless of what the term used to mean, we are all well-aware of what it stands for today. Thus, the practice of being a nice guy has yet another potential problem with the way it sometimes manifests in social interactions. There are some people who will be nice only as a means to an end. What this means is that certain individuals will fake being nice in order to deceive others and get their way through manipulation. This is not a rare occurrence at all, and it clearly shows that simply being nice is far from enough to define a real gentleman. This is where the difference between a gentleman and a masquerading liar becomes apparent.

Being a gentleman is something you cannot fake, it's something that you develop over time, and there are no short ways of doing that. And the good news is that, in spite of modern assumptions, women genuinely enjoy the self-sufficient, self-respected, confident attitude of a real gentleman. Because that never goes out of style.

However, this change won't happen overnight and will begin as your perceptions of life start to expand. In other words, you must become a more open-minded person. You will perceive the world differently, and, in turn, the people around you will convey you more positively. This will bring you the well-deserved respect.

Nowadays, it can be quite difficult to make a good impression and deliver the proper image. This happens in general, not only in relation to women. The typical conceptions our modern society has brought upon us have managed to direct the attention from the attitude of a proper gentleman, towards the image of a so-called modern man, who we no longer can refer to as an honorable individual.

This lack of honor in the contemporary standards of conduct stems primarily from the way we are taught to put ourselves first, to cast notions of chivalry and honesty aside in order to attain personal goals. Honor used to be associated with the highest social circles and nobility once upon a time, and it was held in very high regard by those individuals who stood out as the most accomplished in the crowd. This is no longer the case, as bending the rules, disregarding others, being outright immoral, and cutting corners wherever you go, are choices that are considered to make one's path to success a whole lot easier nowadays. What's more, this kind of conduct is even praised sometimes.

Even so, in this exceptional time of lack of "common sense" and stability, manners and chivalry still count as precious personal traits every person should develop. Now, it's true that the world will often not play by the rules, and I am not necessarily saying you need to blindly obey said rules and always fly straight, even to your own detriment. What I am referring to are some of the more fundamental personal qualities that are starting to seriously lack. These are accountability, staying true to your word, firmness of principle, strength of character, and even dignity among others. It's apparent that many people who have achieved success in our time care very little about such makings of character, and are willing to forgo everything that defines them as long as it gets them closer to the top. This attitude is in stark contrast to being a gentleman.

You may wonder, what is the use of staying true to yourself if being principled will ultimately leave you behind in the race? The answer is – it won't. As you will learn through reading this book, it is entirely possible to be successful, accomplish great things, and attract the attention of women while being a gentleman. Moreover, this approach will yield better and long-lasting results, which we will explore in more detail later on.

Regardless of the changes our society deals with at the moment, being a gentleman should be every self-respected man's way of life. And, contrary to popular view, in spite of your family background, choosing to lead the life of a gentleman is, first and foremost a choice, and, if you were to ask me – the best choice you could make for shaping your character.

The main purpose of this book is to help you learn how to develop the traits of a real gentleman and become a respectable member of our society. While this is important to some extent, I also want to put the emphasis on the importance of this decision for your personal development. Only after you comprehend that this is, first of all, a choice you make for yourself, will you be able to make a positive impression on women and those surrounding you.

This book is a must read for all men out there whether you're a student, a parent, a business person, teacher, a blue collar worker, a sales executive or a specialist in any other domain. It will help you improve yourself. Every self-respected man who yearns for professional and personal success should lead the life of a real gentleman.

It is no secret that the path of a gentleman is sometimes the one of more resistance, but you will find it is more than worth it. After all, a great way to measure whether you are doing it right in life is to take note of the amount of resistance you get from the world as you go about your way. The key, however, is to persevere – and this is one of the cornerstones of every true gentleman's character.

This book is the first step you must take in order to become a better version of yourself. So, start setting up new standards for yourself and you might even give a good example for others as well.

So, congratulations for wanting to learn more about becoming a true gentleman! You have taken the leap towards your self-development! Are you ready? Let's get started!

Chapter 1: G for Generosity

"Generosity lies less in giving much than in giving at the right moment." (Jean de La Bruyère)

Before we proceed further and delve into what it is that constitutes a gentleman in this day and age and how to go about building yourself up into one, we will examine the concept of a gentleman on a more fundamental level.

There exists a multitude of dictionary definitions of the term itself, primarily varying based on context, of course. While the word used to be, and still is at times, ascribed to a person born into a specific circumstance, particularly an individual born into a form of nobility, this is not what we will be focusing on. On the contrary, the primary interest of this book is to look into the concept of a gentleman as defined by his actions, attitude, and general outlook on life and relationships.

This is where a very important split occurs when it comes to defining a gentleman. One definition concerns social status, while the other focuses on behavior and mannerisms. Our interest is in the latter. So, in the simplest possible terms, a gentleman is a man who treats people with a certain level of respect and holds his own behavior to a very high standard of what is considered proper and chivalrous conduct, usually in a traditional sense.

As you can see, this is, by definition, something that can be attained and mastered regardless of your age or circumstance of birth, as it's all about actions and the way you carry yourself. Being a gentleman is a way to live, not just a way to approach women or people in general. By the end of this book, you will have gained insight into how to mold your own character into that of a gentleman.

There are numerous misconceptions with regards to how the life of a real gentleman should be led. One of them is that a gentleman is the description of a soft, weak and not masculine individual – in a nutshell – a wuss.

This couldn't be further from the truth, however, as a real gentleman is a man who is perfectly in touch with his masculinity and exhibits traits that are very male in essence. Such a man will display great confidence and self-control, while still not coming across as self-centered and arrogant. There is a great difference between confidence and vanity, and this simple truth appears to be forgotten more and more as the years go by. As a matter of fact, vanity should often imply a lack of real confidence, as excessive pride of one's self is usually a form of compensation for other shortcomings of character. Still, vanity and arrogance continue to be portrayed as confidence and a show of manliness very often. As a result, when a gentleman who is not boastful, but silently confident and at peace with himself, shows up, he is perceived by some as less assertive, less confident, and, ultimately, less manly. Luckily, people with this point of view are not a vast majority and don't really matter, although they are quite loud at times.

Typically, this general misconception is, to some extent, determined by mass media, and the main ideas it promotes, especially those concerning the relationship between men and women, and the whole concept of feminism that has reached a maximum at the moment.

Leaving aside all the contradictions regarding feminism, even if they say it aloud or not, women like to be treated nicely, with proper attention and undying respect. Such a behavior is certainly one of the keys that will open many doors for you, the man reading this!

You may have noticed that certain voices in the public sphere would even go as far as to say that traditional conduct associated with chivalry is somehow demeaning or discriminatory against women. This usually involves attacks on the simplest of ways in which we show respect for women, such as holding a door for them, letting them go first, paying for their drink, etc. All that is considered gentlemanly is under fire, and some try to put a malicious spin on such behavior, trying to make us believe that treating women as ladies somehow has an ulterior motive.

The media, whether intentionally or unconsciously, promotes a recently developed idea that all social aspects of gender are constructed by society, intentionally that is. The subscribers of this point of view forget, however, that the age-old traditions didn't just come out of thin air, but are based on something much more fundamental. The truth is, a lot of the ways in which we interact between genders are based on nature, instinct, and biological programming. Women are not conditioned by society to respond in a certain way to a man holding a door open for them. Instead, the vast majority of them have a natural inclination towards being flattered.

The unprecedented level of gender equality that the developed world has achieved over the last century should provide fertile soil for the best gender relations yet to grow on, where mutual respect is cherished along with the innocuous differences established by nature itself, with all their inherent beauty. The fact of the matter is that women and men are not the same, and accepting this simple truth in a time of equality is a good thing. This is what every real gentleman acts upon and knows to be true.

The detrimental notions of eradicating gender, though they probably come from a specific source, are often perpetuated unintentionally through various forms of media and can cause great harm to the overall happiness of both the individual and society at large.

Even so, in spite of all these aspects that we unconsciously promote, our relationships are the ones that suffer the most. Without paying serious attention to the way in which we convey a relationship and our behavior, we end up losing interest, and afterward suffer the consequences.

As you'll learn while you go on reading, there are plenty of ways in which you can bolster your understanding of others, especially women. Most importantly, you must learn to properly communicate, listen, and impress.

Don't get confused and frustrated saying that women are indecipherable beings. This might be accurate to some extent (I'm in the same place as you are), but this is one of the traits that makes them irresistible to us, isn't it? For this reason, you have to take on a gentleman's armor, and you'll be on the right path. One of the main traits you need to shape as a worthy gentleman is generosity, as the name of this chapter already implies. Having the same initial as the magical word – gentleman – we will deal with it first.

Learn when to be generous

Every self-respected gentleman has to acknowledge the thin line between being flashy and slightly inappropriate with a fake, over the top generosity, and the precise meaning of the word. A man who is generous will know when to offer to pay the bill, as the evening ends, and be subtle about it, not flash the gesture so that everybody takes notice of his immense generosity. He will know when it's the right timing to send his wife or girlfriend a token of his appreciation – whether we're talking about a bouquet of flowers or a beautiful piece of jewelry.

I will tell you what a generous man will never do – take the woman of his dreams to the most expensive restaurant in the city and afterward complain or brag about the bill. And, most importantly, a gentleman won't overwhelm a girl with multiple over the top gifts, which are utterly expensive, after just a couple of dates.

What it all boils down to is realizing that generosity is never about the person showing it, but about the person receiving it. This seems fairly obvious, and yet, it is incredible how often people forget this core aspect of the concept of generosity.

Many use what only appears as generosity on the surface with the aim to boost their own ego and show off, thus defeating the whole point of generosity altogether. A rich man and a poor man can both be equally generous, as generosity is measured by intent more than anything else. Needless to say, the less material means a person has, the more powerful his gestures of generosity become.

I hope you get the picture. Generosity is not about portraying that you have large amounts of cash at your disposal, and you are willing to spend them whenever you want. On the contrary, generosity is expressed when a real gentleman notices that he should help whenever a person he knows is in need of it. These are some of the gestures that can be linked to authentic generosity, the personality trait you have to develop.

I don't doubt that you are acquainted with Jane Austen's famous novel "Pride and Prejudice." While perhaps it is not your all-time favorite read, you are pretty much aware of the storyline, am I right? Mr. Darcy, one of the leading characters in the novel, is one of the most popular male figures in British literature, and that has remained unchanged. If you were to ask any woman if she knew who Mr. Darcy was, you would be surprised of her reaction!

The greater majority of women dream of men like Mr. Darcy, who are the steering image of authentic chivalry, generosity, and other equally attractive character traits. Contrary to what you might assume, Mr. Darcy was anything but a prince charming, if we were to refer to his appearance. If not, what is it that made him so popular among ladies all over the world? One of the main features that convinced Miss Elizabeth Bennet that Mr. Darcy was worth her time was generosity. Yes, you heard that right!

Darcy's authentic, sheer generosity, directed towards everyone surrounding him, whether we're talking about his family, friends or enemies, was the single aspect that shaped his character. After perceiving the generous nature of Darcy's character, Elizabeth conveyed him from a different perspective, and fell in love with him, and she's not the only one, as numerous other women have fallen for him as well (while reading the novel, of course).

If you're the type of guy who is rather cheap, and you think twice before paying the bill to a nice dinner date, you'd better rethink your approach. I have no doubt that almost every woman yearns to be indulged and pampered. That doesn't necessarily imply that you should surround her with flowers and expensive presents that scream generosity. But it definitely wouldn't hurt if you offered to pay the bill from time to time, and make the gesture appear as natural as possible! And, please remember, don't flash your generosity. I want to point that generosity isn't necessarily about money, but about the gesture and the neat intention of making your date feel spoiled and appreciated.

On the other hand, remember never to be forceful. You may end up surprised by the number of women who not only don't expect their dinner and drinks to be paid for every time but actually want to pay the bill themselves or at least split it between the two of you. This is becoming increasingly more normal nowadays. However, always seize the opportunity to be generous and indulge in traditional conduct by taking the charge, especially at the start of a relationship. Unless you meet resistance from her side, go ahead and take care of the bill.

The truth is that modern times may indeed be a bit more complicated than the ways of the past. There is more diversity in our society now than ever before, and this holds true for the female population as well, of course. This is why it may prove difficult, or impossible, to concoct the perfect approach that is sure to please and impress every person you encounter. This is not a bad thing, mind you, it's quite the contrary. More diversity means more choice and more possibilities. But the beautiful thing about being a gentleman is that it is the most foolproof way of life if you strive to establish meaningful and valuable contact with others, most of all women. The nature of a gentleman is such that he is not too loud, not too imposing, and certainly not a pusher. His character traits are the most neutral when it comes to the kinds of reactions he evokes in people.

Every woman has her set of expectations concerning the relationship with a man. And every time you somehow don't accomplish fulfilling that set of expectations, on an unconscious level, she will start to resent you for making her compromise her standards. You might not pay attention to small details like these, but if your attitude and approach towards the woman in your life displays a sheer disregard for her expectations, you are this close to being left alone. On the other hand, though, if you can work on your manners and try to educate yourself by implementing generosity and other features into your conduct, you will have so much more to offer, and this will alter your relationship entirely.

Of course, if you are after establishing a meaningful relationship with someone special, you want to seek out a woman that does have high standards. The problem with this breed is that some men may be discouraged to try harder when they encounter a woman that has her standards set high. This is not the way of a gentleman, as he reacts in the opposite way. The standards of the one he sets his sights on will encourage him to do better and improve himself, not seek out an easier alternative.

How to show your generosity?

I would like to expand a little bit more on this. I already said that generosity doesn't necessarily imply making obvious remarks about how much money you have. On the contrary, generosity is more about the little things. It's about your undivided attention towards her, the time you are willing to put aside for her sake – in a nutshell, your capability of making priorities.

For instance, during a conversation, you can actually portray your generosity. You might ask – how is that possible? It is possible! Yes, by directing the conversation towards her, instead of talking about yourself nonstop. Of course, that doesn't mean you should say nothing and stare at the ceiling.

This is very important. Most of us actually have a natural impulse to talk about ourselves, and the conversation can thus quickly get derailed and become entirely focused on you. You may not do it on purpose, of course, or even notice it, but it will make you appear as if you are full of yourself. Worse yet, some people will actually spin every single thing their partner in conversation says and try to make it revolve around them, instead of listening to the other person. For example, a woman you are talking to may begin a story that reminds you of some past experience you had, and your story may indeed be very interesting as well, but you need to resist the urge to share everything and jump into the conversation right away.

She may begin telling you about a bad experience she had at a certain restaurant, for instance, and if it so happens that you went there too, you may get the urge to jump in with something like "Oh, the same thing happened to me when I went there. It was then, there, and with him, etc." And before you know it, you have completely turned the flow of the conversation around and have cast her story aside. Save your story for later or for an entirely different occasion even, as you don't want to snatch her spotlight and go on and on about yourself. This is a very annoying habit that a lot of people have, which manifests in many conversations, regardless of the type of company in question. It is definitely not the mark of a gentleman. Being a good listener and someone a woman enjoys talking to entails patience, self-control, focus, and, most of all, respect.

The bottom line is that generosity is portrayed in everything you do. And as you walk with the woman you like, you should pay attention to what she says, and remember what she's telling you. Be interested in whatever she has to say, and make her feel important. This is how a woman should feel in the presence of a gentleman – significant and appreciated.

Furthermore, other people's feelings and points of view should always be taken into consideration by a real gentleman. I know, I know – you might be saying – "why should I care more about other people's feelings instead of my own? I won't permit anyone to dictate what I should do or how I should behave." But, is this really the kind of attitude that you wish to adopt?

Typically, the foundation of this modern approach is the culture we live in – a Me-centered culture, which teaches us to care about our feelings and emotions first and foremost. This is the society that, in a way or another, shapes our character and influences us. In a world in which generosity and respect are values that are almost extinct, you need to stand out and embrace another attitude!

The root of all problems is, in many cases, an elevated view of your own person. Try to foster an attitude of empathy, which will show that you care about other persons as well. Thus, try treating those surrounding you as you wish to be treated. I will develop more on this subject later in the book.

I mentioned that generosity lies in your ability to prioritize. I want to clarify this subject a bit. By prioritizing, I mean that you should place her needs ahead of yours. Of course, you have to spend some time with the boys every once in a while to watch a game and chill with a glass of cold beer, but how about restraining from this when it's your anniversary or her birthday? On such occasions, you should put her first, and take the time to plan something special she will appreciate, which will win her heart!

Generosity has nothing to do with money, but it is a man's most valuable behavioral trait. In simpler words, you need to make it become part of you, and, in time, it will come naturally. You don't have to aim at altering your behavior overnight, but with little, basic changes, you'll manage to become the man every woman dreams of.

It's okay to take it very slow at first. Try to bear what you have learned in mind at all times and then identify a small situation that gives you an opportunity to try your new approach. Do a small thing a little differently than you would have before, show at least the smallest amount of generosity where you otherwise wouldn't, and then take it from there as you become more and more generous over time. You'd be surprised by how easily being generous can become a thing of habit.

Begin by polishing your actions, thoughts and, try to give more often! After you start implementing these little changes into your everyday life, things will alter. Soon, it will become second nature, and you will have managed to live by new, cavalry standards. This character trait will be portrayed in your behavior towards your family, friends, lady friends and even enemies. You will be amazed by the way in which you will be conveyed by your fellow friends due to the improvement in your actions.

Chapter 2: E for Etiquette

"A gentleman is someone who does not what he wants to do, but what he should do." (Haruki Murakami)

If I were to ask you to tell me the first word that pops into your mind when you think of a gentleman, it would certainly be etiquette. Am I right? Etiquette is, possibly, one of the crucial character traits a gentleman will develop to perfection. To perceive himself with self-respect, while at the same time being respectful and considerate of other people's thoughts and opinions, to be chivalrous but never exaggerated in words and actions, and, always – always present a set of exquisite manners.

The word "etiquette" is usually linked to immaculate white handkerchiefs and courtesies, and multiple forks and spoons lined on the table. To some extent, manners are associated with such aspects as well. Probably, this is one of the reasons you don't feel attracted to this type of restaurants that require impeccable manners on your behalf. Meanwhile, chilling in front of the baseball game with a cold beer in your hand doesn't require any attention or effort.

However, sometimes, the woman in your life might highly appreciate your effort of taking her to a nice dinner, and make her feel like a princess. Think of it as a chance to turn yourself into a man who is more versatile, which a gentleman surely is. There is absolutely nothing wrong with the aforementioned activities that you may enjoy, but then again, there is nothing wrong with learning to carry yourself in a different environment either.

Becoming a gentleman is your opportunity of improving yourself. I don't mean that you need to go back to school in order to polish your mannerism skills and the way in which you behave. But, it is crucial that every individual has a set of standards to live by. You should always look to broaden your horizons in any possible way; this is how you will get more out of life, and it will surely do you no harm. What's more, women will appreciate a man who can handle any given situation or place where she may find herself with him. This is why your behavior and what's on the inside are so important, because no matter how you dress and present yourself on the outside, you will stick out in certain places as long as you lack the proper manners. More often than not, manners really do make a man.

You may have encountered situations in which you were treated poorly and rudely. How did that situation make you feel? And would it have made a difference if the person you are thinking of were dressed elegantly? Of course not! See where I'm headed? It doesn't matter whether a person is dressed immaculately or not, as long as he doesn't behave politely, as a gentleman should. For instance, let's say that you have a car, which no longer functions properly. Regardless of the amount of time you spend polishing and washing the exterior, that wouldn't change the fact that it doesn't work.

In a world that typically comprises of men who lack respect one for another; a gentleman will stand out of the crowd – courteous, considerate and kind. The way in which you choose to behave in the presence of others is, literally, your personification. You needn't say much, as your actions speak for yourself. If your behavior displays respect, then, you will be treated with respect in return.

This too is one of the most important traits a gentleman has – his actions and conduct speak volumes about his person. The less you say and the more you do, the more respect people will have for you. A gentleman will not verbally point out to others that he is generous, chivalrous or kind; he will instead conduct himself in a way that directly shows all of these qualities.

Manners may seem old-fashioned to some, but that is certainly not true. Good manners are treasured even in today's world, and will never go out of style. However, don't get me wrong. Being a well-mannered individual doesn't mean that you are supposed to be an uptight guy who is unable to enjoy himself and have some fun. Because manners don't have anything to do with pleasure. They are all about respect – towards yourself and towards the people you come in contact with. Period.

In some cases, people would associate an individual who doesn't have a respectful set of manners as having a bad character. Don't let the world around you make you become an irresponsible man who lacks common sense and manners. Begin every day with a positive attitude, and soon, this way of living will become part of you.

Before we get into the details of a gentleman's etiquette, it's important to note that there is a certain truth of life that has stood as long as civilization itself, and it appears to be relevant nowadays more than ever. This truth is that the harder you try to better yourself and adhere to your principles, the more pushback you will get from people in general. That is because being a gentleman takes effort and dedication, something that a lot of people are neither willing nor capable to put in, and thus when they see a man successfully adopting such a way of life it reminds them of their own shortcoming. This makes some of them spiteful and insecure. Some will even throw hurdles your way and try to persuade you to be more like everyone else so that you stop disrupting their comfort in the way they live.

It depends, however, on the kind of people you surround yourself with. You need to make sure that those close to you have an equally strong will for self-improvement. Otherwise, your alternative is to simply persevere and go against the current, which can get quite tiresome. This kind of problem is present among young people more than anywhere else, where peer pressure is the most intense. A man may find himself in an environment that has no respect for values such as generosity and honor, and it can be incredibly hard for him to stay true to himself when everyone around him is constantly doing the opposite and applying pressure on him at the same time. The key is to be confident in what you are and what you want to be, assure yourself that you are right and hold your own, and if this means a little bit of pride, then so be it.

However, assuming that you don't have to face conflict concerning morality and deep convictions on a daily basis, we'll examine the more external and simple makings of a gentleman's appearance and posture for the time being. Now, let's have a closer look at what does etiquette refer to.

Appearance

"Fashion can be bought. Style one must possess." – Edna Woolman Chase

Can you think of a gentleman who is sloppy in appearance? Certainly not. Remaining classy and elegant throughout the day should be among every self-respected man's priorities. Your style is the translucent mirror reflecting your personality and is as subjective as it can get.

A lot of men want to look different, and the thought of changing your style may seem to you like you're trying to become someone that you're not. But, the truth is that you can dress for success like a real gentleman, and add a little bit of personality to your outfits. If you are like the greater majority of men, at the moment you might think of this gentleman idea with an unexplained unease. But, it's understandable, as the change doesn't come without any efforts.

Paying attention to any detail regarding your clothing goes a long way, especially when we're talking about first impressions. The way you dress is clearly important in portraying your behavior. Outfits are often viewed as an imperative aspect of non-verbal communication, which will have a significant impact on the way in which other people will see you. Your appearance will portray your confidence, culture, age, interest, and value.

Now, let's see the main pillars you should take into consideration concerning your style.

Fit

A gentleman's clothes will fit his body perfectly. Yes, yes, you need to stop dressing like a teenager, as if you didn't surpass that phase of your life. I want to tell you that oversized clothing equals sloppy and can even portray you as slightly immature. Period.

I know that if you look around you, you'll imminently notice two extremes —men who dress in oversized clothes that make them appear as if they are Tupac's brothers, or men that are dressed similarly to women. You get the picture, don't you?

But, typically, men have a natural inclination towards wearing clothes that are at least two sizes larger than their actual size. Try to avoid that. This style is anything but flattering, and it doesn't help you look young but ridiculous. A sloppy appearance will only display that you don't care.

For instance, if you finally managed to schedule a date with the woman you have set your eyes on, and you show up underdressed, you will make a bad first impression on your lady friend, I assure you!

As a hint, you should know that the clothes you wear should almost hug your body. But don't get me wrong, this definitely doesn't mean that you should wear tight clothes. There is a thin line between fit and tight, and a self-respected man should not cross it. The core to looking your best is finding the balance in this direction, and dressing in a way that flatters your body.

Simplicity

Simplicity is another golden rule for every self-respected gentleman. The way you dress shouldn't be your primary way of expressing yourself. It is true that our dress code portrays to some extent who we are, but you shouldn't let this be of crucial importance.

For this reason, develop simplicity and elegance. You needn't draw attention only to the way you dress, and you shouldn't turn to funky jewelry or flashy accessories to stand out of the crowd. If you were a woman, would you date a guy who wears more accessories and dresses more colorful than you? One who has three rings on one finger, shiny bracelets on each hand and a fluorescent t-shirt? Of course you wouldn't date such a person. The perfect image of this man is a pure exaggeration and lack of style.

By all means, what I wish to outline is that you need to find your style, see what you're comfortable with, and embrace it. Of course, it's great to add a stylish watch to your outfit or a high-quality pair of shoes, but wearing every accessory you own at a time is certainly not recommendable.

Nonchalant

A gentleman knows how to wear his clothes with particular nonchalance. He will look relaxed, in spite of the elegant clothes he is wearing. However, a casual look is anything but dull, and a gentleman is not afraid to develop his own style.

Don't be scared to experiment, and wear plenty of collared shirts, vests, sweaters so on and so forth. Let's say that for the fall season, instead of opting for an oversized hoodie, you choose a beautiful, wool knitted sweater. This will indeed look much better, and give you a more gentlemanlike look. And don't hesitate to experiment with blazers, as they're very versatile.

The importance of color

You shouldn't underestimate the color power carries when picking out an outfit. Particular colors grab the attention while some are bringing to light other pieces of clothing. Also, you should settle what suits your skin tone and style best, because maybe not every color suits you.

Also, you should decide what message you wish to convey through your outfit. If you want to transmit a message showing authority and self-confidence, then wearing a classic combination of dark navy and red will do the trick. On the other hand, a man who would rather go for an outfit in earthly tones will display openness and positivity. For this reason, settle what type of personality you would like to convey, and only afterward construct your wardrobe.

Dress for the occasion

Some men are resistant towards dressing according to a particular event because they feel that the rest of the men will be dressed casually and they'll feel over the top. But bear this in mind, if the people you know don't pay attention to the way in which they dress, that doesn't mean you should do the same.

Remember, the little things are the ones that make the difference. Wearing a beautiful suit to a wedding will differentiate yourself from the rest of the crowd wearing casual shirts. And also, don't be afraid to include little details to your outfit, which will indicate your style. For instance, a basic, yet statement accessory such as a watch, or a pocket square can genuinely make an impression.

Less is more

You surely know this particular expression. I know it's a cliché, but it's 100 percent true! Dressing nicely doesn't mean that all your money should be directed towards purchasing clothes. A gentleman has to develop his ability to opt for quality over quantity. Having lots of clothes shouldn't be your priority, but it's important to shop for pieces that survive the test of time and look good on you, and, most importantly, are high-qualitative.

For instance, make sure that your wardrobe encompasses a positive collection of shirts in various neutral colors, as well as patterned ones that will add some spice to your outfits.

Dressing professionally enhances self-discipline

Another perk that comes with dressing professionally is that it will contribute to improving your self-discipline. Typically, a gentleman will anticipate what he will be doing throughout the day, and only afterward will he select the clothing items according to that. Also, a gentleman will know how to meet various dressing requirements, appearing elegantly at the same time.

First impressions

The truth is that people have always judged other people based on their appearance, and that's not about to change anytime soon. In this direction, a first impression is made in less than three seconds, and the next 90 seconds will settle whether that impression is the right one or not. In simpler words, this means that in less than a couple of minutes, our impression on someone is cut in stone before that person even opens his/her mouth. For this reason, anyone should pay attention to the importance of dressing professionally and neatly.

At the moment, we live in a society in which the greater majority of men have a natural inclination towards dressing down. Most men settle for a pair of jeans, a t-shirt and sneakers. If you aim at improving your style, this will help you stand out of the crowd.

A first impression is made in a matter of seconds. And, even though there are cases in which they don't come to our advantage, first impressions are powerful, and will have a significant influence on the opinion a person will form on you. For this reason, it is crucial that you pay attention to the message your clothes convey. Because sometimes, they speak louder than your words.

You know that saying "don't judge a book by its covers", don't you? Even though we are all aware of it, to some extent, we are highly influenced by the covers of a book, as well as the appearance of an individual. What would you prefer? To have someone say about you – "he is dressed like an authentic gentleman" or "he looks like an irresponsible individual"?

I'm not saying that appearance is the most important aspect about a person. Not at all. But, it does matter a lot, and in a world described by competition, it is common sense to comprehend the importance of clothing and grooming.

Ultimately, while it's true that what's on the inside is more important in the long run, this does not mean that appearance is irrelevant. The clue is in the order of things when establishing a new relationship with someone. Namely, looks are important because they are, in most cases, what kick-starts a relationship and what instigates interest in someone. We are very visual creatures, especially us men, so looks matter a lot and should be given attention as they open the door for what follows.

Now, after conversation begins, what's on the inside of you comes into play. And if it's no good, your appearance may become completely irrelevant. Some relationships can start and even go on for a while based solely on external attraction, but sooner or later, your character will determine how long and how intense the connection with someone will be. Speaking strictly in terms of relationships with women, physical attraction and passion are strong factors, but they start to dilute after a few months when our brains begin to cool down after the initial infatuation. That's when you need something more meaningful to keep the fire going, and this means character, understanding, and a connection on a much deeper level.

Think of your appearance as just the tip of the iceberg that is your whole person; it's important and the most visible, but it's far from the full picture. Both what's on the surface and what's below are important, so you have to work on both. This concept of balance applies to much more than just successful relationships; it's also important in other walks of life. So, cherish your inner qualities, but never underestimate the effect that a well-groomed appearance can produce and the doors it can open for you.

"Clothes don't make a man, but clothes have got many a man a good job." – Unknown

Presence

Now, after we've talked about appearance, I wish to draw your attention towards the importance of presence. This is entirely distinctive from appearance if that's what you were thinking.

Please answer this question: did you ever carry a conversation with a person who made you feel as if what you were saying is utterly boring? I bet you have. But how did it make you feel? I bet you didn't feel over the moon, did you?

What this means, among other things, is that you need to be responsive and attentive when you're having a conversation with somebody, especially women. Men often forget that girls too are self-conscious, often even more so than us. When a woman is telling you a story or anything of the sort, you must focus and respond actively to her. This way, she will feel that what she has to say interests you, thus also knowing that you are interested in her. It will make her feel more at ease and more comfortable around you, and that is very important, especially if you met recently and are only beginning to date.

Beware that you don't get pushed to the sidelines, though, as some women, and people in general, really like to talk way too much. Being responsive can also help you avoid this and stay in the conversation so that it doesn't become her monolog for the next twenty minutes. Most people who talk a lot don't get carried away on purpose, and it's more of a habit than anything else. So, don't be quick to hold it against them. Instead, you can respond strategically and thus guide the conversation towards a more equal level.

It appears that fewer and fewer men are now able to carry a conversation and be 100 percent present. Let's be honest, every one of us is, to some extent, a bit narcissist when it comes to this aspect.

Nowadays, smartphones have become a big part of our daily lives, which makes being 100 percent present significantly harder. I bet you know what I'm talking about! People aim at dividing their attention into two separate directions, the real, palpable world, and the virtual world. The all-time window towards this cyber world is, of course, our phones. If you were to pay attention to a typical American restaurant, you would notice that the greater majority of people stare at their cell phones during dinner instead of interacting with one another. It's a sad, yet true reality.

Being present during a date, meeting, or any other social event, may be difficult, even though it appears to be a simple concept. And as hard as you tried to look present, if you're always staring at the phone or browsing on Facebook, it's pointless; you can't fake it.

But, I would like to tell you that you can make a difference, and convey presence. However, it will imply a lot of determination and willpower on your behalf, but if you truly concentrate on directing your attention towards being present, you will be able to do it, eventually.

The difficulty of doing away with this rude habit lies in your mental processes, though, not in the physical effort required. Technically, there's nothing simpler than putting your phone on silent and leaving it in your jacket or wherever on the side. The trick is to understand that you probably don't have to be available to every single person, at every single point in your day. A gentleman is a self-respecting individual, and he thus values his own time as well. Believe me, the vast majority of well-adjusted people won't be offended that you didn't text them back for half an hour after they contacted you. And if they mention it later and try to hold it against you, simply tell the truth – you were with someone and were indisposed at the moment. They'll just have to learn to live with it.

This is how you manage your time and availability, helping you to focus on being present when spending time with someone you care about. Just make sure that they are responding to your behavior in kind, though.

On the other hand, you should understand that being with one person at a time is often enough, especially if they matter to you. Learn to focus on the person before you and disregard your other contacts for at least a little while. A man who will point his attention towards his phone shows that he is insecure, and even needy. On the contrary, a true gentleman acknowledges that the continuous and annoying use of his smartphone shows that he doesn't cherish, nor respect the person he is with.

Conversation

So we've talked about the crucial importance of being present, but what about conversation? How does a true gentleman behave when conversing with another person?

Certainly, your conversational skills are essential in establishing contact with another individual. Plus, conversation counts as an important point when it comes to a gentleman's manners.

I have to tell you that asking a woman how her day went is not enough if that's what you thought! If, after asking her about her day, you begin enumerating all sorts of things that you've been doing, directing the conversation towards your person, then the first question was in vain. This denotes sheer narcissism, and you should avoid this at all costs. I was telling you before about the importance of generosity, and how it can be portrayed in simple little things such as the art of conversation. Remember, right?

A woman will be increasingly more interested in establishing a connection with you if you portray interest and generosity in your approach. In order to achieve that, you need to find out about one another, what interests you share. Are you with me?

In this direction, it's genuinely important that you speak with confidence and as politely as possible. A proper speech will show people that you care. Typically, a lot of men make use of profanity because politeness doesn't matter too much to them. And you might fall into this trap as well – "if everyone around me is doing so, why should I behave any differently?" But this shouldn't be your way of thinking. Everyone of us can learn how to become a better person, in this case, a gentleman. And learning isn't something that we can only associate with school; it's a never-ending process that helps us grow into better persons.

A gentleman will always be polite, and will avoid speaking loudly or yelling, even when the conversation he has is a contradictory one. If you have a natural inclination towards being overly loud, then you need to pay increased attention to this detail and try to speak more quietly. Trust me, people won't have trouble hearing you.

Chapter 3: N for the No's

"Anyone can be heroic from time to time, but a gentleman is something you have to be all the time." - Luigi Pirandello

I would like to aim your attention on the No's. This way, it will become clearer to you what is keeping you from becoming a real gentleman, and being with the woman of your dreams. Being a real gentleman isn't necessarily linked to positive actions only; you also need to get acquainted with some of the main things you should stay away from! Are you ready? Follow me.

Being self-absorbed

Every man reading this book knows that, deep within us, we have a slight tendency of being self-absorbed. It's true, and it's no use denying it. And this is certainly no news for you, as this is one of the primary character traits of the greater majority of men! This particular tendency has something to do with the way in which our society works, but that's another subject, and we're not going to delve into it now.

However, a real gentleman doesn't expect the world to revolve around his narcissist personality, as much as you'd like that to be true. And as you're reading this book, and wish to develop your character, you should know that this is a definite NO, and women find this kind of attitude unattractive and unappealing.

To be fair, it's not just that our society promotes this kind of attitude. It's also a thing of nature to be primarily focused on ourselves and our own perspective, and this only makes matters worse. Even if you happen to be the most considerate guy alive, the chances are that you are still going to be self-absorbed to a certain extent. This is alright, though, as we can't help but perceive the world through our own eyes. The trick, once again, is to find a balance and put in the effort needed to do better.

A good way to practice being less egocentric in the beginning is to simply ask a lot of questions. This is not a hard thing to do, especially if you are with a woman who you find to be interesting. Start simple by asking her how her day was or how she's doing, and then follow up on that with related questions accordingly. Most of the time, when someone tells you something, there is room for further questions on the topic, if you pay attention that is.

You'll find that most people, women especially, really like to see you show interest in this way. After a while, you are bound not only to come across as less self-absorbed but to start experiencing an honest change within you as well. Keep in mind that a lot of modern women are very career-oriented and ambitious, so there is a lot going on in their lives. Just like you, they too like to talk about themselves and whatever may be happening to them at the time.

If you are committed to making a change in your life, and I believe you are, then you need to educate yourself and try to eliminate this inborn tendency of being self-absorbed. As I've stated before, it's crucial to keep the conversation flowing both ways so that a woman will feel equal, or even in the lead.

Allow me to give you an example. During a conversation you have with a woman you are attracted to, pay attention to the number of times you include the personal pronouns "I", "me", "my". If it seems that you're the only one talking, and all she does is nodding or agreeing to your affirmations, I must tell you, this is not right. Even if the girl is, at the time, putting off with your egocentrism, this will only be the source of numerous other frustrations, and your relationship will end badly sooner or later.

The thoughts that go through the mind of the woman conversing with such a narcissist are not happy, positive ones, my friend! She's not saying to herself – "I believe I have finally found the guy who comprehends and appreciates me." If she is nice enough to listen to your "sermons", that only means she is friendly and polite!

Besides coming across as egocentric, you will also appear as though you crave too much attention, which is probably one of the most unattractive traits a man can have. Needless to say, this is the polar opposite of the kind of attitude a gentleman must project.

You can indeed aim at fixing this type of attitude, no doubt. As long as you wish to do that, of course. And you need to start with little fundamental changes, which will come naturally in time. For instance, try to learn more about the woman you are dating. And always be considerate of her feelings and respect her principles and ideas.

Being late and unreliable

Punctuality is a constructive habit every self-respected man should develop. It indicates that you have an upstanding character and respect your word. Plus, being punctual genuinely contributes to constructing your self-confidence. It will show the person you are meeting with that you are a trustworthy individual, and they can depend on you on no matter the situation. If you say that you'll meet someone at a particular time, and you appear late, this means that you have broken your promise, and that's not the attitude you wish to convey, is it?

A gentleman's word is his bond, and this is one of his signature characteristics. When he says that he will be at a place at a particular time, people know for certain that it will be so. You need to foster this kind of attitude at all times and with all matters in life, even if someone else doesn't reciprocate. If a person you're supposed to meet doesn't show up on time, don't be vindictive. Instead, maintain your punctuality and their conscience will do the rest. No well-adjusted person, whether they are a man or a woman, will want to always run late to meet someone who is always on time for them.

Once a woman notices that you pay deep attention to being always on time, she will feel highly appreciated, as if you truly cherish the time with her, and you don't wish to spend any second of that time by being late. In a way, it's definitely not a mistake to say that punctuality is an attractive quality, especially in a man!

Being punctual regardless of the situation will show that you are a disciplined fellow, who organizes his time most attentively, and doesn't perceive life as an accident. Furthermore, we can say that punctuality is a simple mirror portraying your profound respect towards the person you meet.

And in a way, being late is similar to stealing someone's time. When your actions make others wait for you and lose time, you are actually robbing those people of 10, 15, 20 minutes of their lives! Punctuality indicates that you convey time as truly significant, and you don't wish to waste it.

In a nutshell, being late will hurt your relationships, and your professional career as well. In this direction, plenty of companies present strict policies concerning punctuality.

Of course, keeping your word is also just as important outside of showing up on time for appointments. When you say you will do something, do it. Otherwise, don't make promises and keep in mind that it's always better to turn someone down than make a promise you won't end up keeping. I don't know about you, but I have encountered many a man who will always jump to make a promise that turns out empty. The type of guy who always has everybody "covered" but never delivers on anything. You most likely know the type.

No man alive is a hundred percent dependable with all matters in life. This is why it's important to know your weaknesses and always be aware of what you can and cannot make happen. A gentleman exhibits great self-awareness at all times. This means that if someone asks you for a favor, and you are unsure that you can accommodate them, then just politely say no.

This is also a form of being dependable when you think about it. You want people to be able to depend on you being honest and straightforward and not waste their time. A broken promise causes much greater disappointment than straight up denying someone right away.

Being rude

Typically, there's no situation in which being rude is excusable. And of course, as I already outlined, a gentleman will be careful to behave attentively with everybody he gets in contact with, not only with the woman he likes. And this includes the people whom he doesn't find genuinely appealing.

If you try to be nice to your lady friend, and afterward, the waiter brings you the wrong order, and you act rudely, that will only show that you are a hypocrite, and the behavior you try to display towards your date, is, in fact, a lie. Sometimes, it's difficult to be quiet when you are mistreated, or a service is not carried out as it should be, I know. But, in spite of all this, a gentleman can hold his temper, and show the same amount of respect towards everyone he gets in contact with, including the rude waiter.

You can tell a whole lot about a man from the way he treats those he doesn't depend on, such as those who serve his drinks and meals, or employees in any establishment in general. When a man has nothing to gain from interacting with an individual, especially when that individual is in the lower ranks of any kind, the man's true nature and character come to light. Women pay very close attention to this, believe me. If you're disrespectful towards such individuals, she will know your attitude with her is just for show because you want something out of her.

There are men who take this horrible approach with people as a default really, which is the worst thing you can do. They are rude and arrogant even when it's completely uncalled for and unprovoked, simply because they perceive others to be below them somehow. A gentleman will be considerate, kind, and polite with personnel that happens to serve him at the time. Thank the waiter when he brings your order and be pleasant, this will make the woman you are with feel more comfortable as well. And if they somehow inconvenience you by making a mistake, you should be tolerant and cut them some slack as their jobs are incredibly hard. Personally, I wouldn't get too worked up even if a waiter or waitress ruined my favorite shirt by accident, let alone if my steak was a bit overcooked. It just happens sometimes, and it certainly wasn't on purpose.

Of course, servers may be rude themselves at times. And again, this is no reason for you to fly off the handle either. Play it cool even when they don't provide the best service. Not only will you leave a good impression on your partner in this way, but you will also assume a moral high ground, which is yet another mark of a gentleman.

Gossiping

Gossip is one of the most disturbing habits, portraying sheer frustration and lack of respect towards others, and yourself as well. Class gives the clear distinction between a real gentleman and a fake one. If you create yourself the image of a person who likes making jokes about almost anyone you meet, your appearance will suffer, that's a given. Gossip is never excusable, and this habit indicates that your interest is directed towards someone else's personal affairs. This also shows you are awfully intrusive. Typically, there's no situation in which gossip is permitted, and this is a golden rule every respectable gentleman should abide by.

There are certain stereotypes that would have you believe gossiping is something primarily done by women. This could not be any further from the truth. Men can get just as bad, if not worse when it comes to spreading rumors and talking behind someone's back. Stereotypes are irrelevant, though, as gossiping is neither girly nor manly – it is simply a low and nasty thing for any human being to do. Why waste time on indulging in gossip talk that does nobody any good when you can spend that time having a meaningful conversation with someone you care about or working on self-improvement? The people who spend all their time intensely looking at other people's affairs usually have quite a mess in their own backyard.

Ultimately, gossiping very clearly points out, for all to see, that the person who indulges in such behavior is highly dissatisfied with their own life above all else, which is why they pay so much attention to the affairs of others.

Not learning to say no

In your speech, there are multiple words and phrases you should steer clear of using at all costs. For instance, the greater majority of Americans use the word "like" numerous times, as well as other expressions that show a limited vocabulary. You should aim at eliminating such expressions, which are juvenile and will build you a negative look.

Plus, I would like to tell you that bathroom jokes or other similar aspects should be avoided at all costs; these will always denote the wrong impression and will display pure immaturity. In the same direction, real gentlemen must avoid swearing, regardless of the situation. Also, sexual jokes and observations that mock other people's religious and political inclinations show lack of common sense.

Such a behavior will always display a lack of self-control and self-discipline. Typically, profanity is used by those who don't have an eloquent speech and don't even try to express their feelings in another way because it's not cool in other people's view.

Remember that language always gives you away. The way you speak is one of the crucial factors in how people perceive you. Of course, if you find yourself in the company of close and very familiar people, you will have a more relaxed attitude just like them, as there is no need to be stuck up. Mannerism in language primarily applies to meeting new people, being surrounded by a wider circle, and maintaining professional relationships. In simpler terms, those environments where leaving an impression is the imperative, are the ones where you'd be well-advised to use appropriate and polite language.

Another important thing to consider is that your language, especially the jokes that you make, are often reflective of your unconscious mind. This means that you will also reflect anything that may be lurking in that part of you and this means your primal inclinations and insecurities, among other things. This is why it's important to watch what you say and joke about.

Also, last but not least, learn that interrupting other people while speaking is a rude gesture, and shows that you have no respect whatsoever towards what the other person is trying to say. This is yet another instance where implementing the golden rule goes a long way towards being a gentleman. You don't like it when someone interrupts you and disregards what you are saying, so don't show such disrespect to others either.

In a nutshell, as you begin paying increased attention to your language, you will notice that things are slowly, yet steadily improving. Still, you have to refine your speech continually. Only teenagers will assume that it's cool to use the same five words over and over again, so don't fall into this mindset. You shouldn't seek credibility in this kind of people. Don't limit your opportunities, and try to comprehend that the world is a big place – there are many people and many opportunities awaiting you, as long as you want to reach them and expand your horizon and vocabulary.

Chapter 4: T for Taking It Slow

"Let's take it slow even though I have fallen; for you are too amazing, and the feelings are too real to rush into this long journey; and though it is tempting, we will be fine; for we have our whole lives to laugh and talk as we travel roads not taken, creating memories that will always be there when the years decline and memories fade."- Nate Tulay

This is one of the key points most men fail to pay attention to. Possibly, it's one of the things we are worst at – taking it slow. Whether you like to accept it or not, deep down, you know that what I'm saying is 100 percent true, don't you? As long as we admit it, we can aim at altering our way of thinking and our behavior, so begin by doing that!

Of course, we are talking about the patience in waiting for the relationship to turn sexual here. If you are looking to establish a meaningful, long-term relationship with a woman, I have to tell you that you need to look for a certain type. Most women who want such a relationship will take it slow in the beginning, exactly for the purpose of seeing whether you are going to stick around or not. You should think of this as a sort of trial of your commitment to her, and if you've found the right woman for you, it is well worth it to pass this trial.

You should strive to connect with her on a mental level before anything else, as this is what a solid relationship is founded upon. Now, don't get the wrong picture, there is nothing wrong with raw physical attraction, which is really another crucial part of a successful relationship. However, the problem with a lot of people, particularly men, is that they overlook everything else. Lust can truly take a hold over a man, but it is more or less transient and tends to subside after a while. This is where the problems begin to occur if a connection on an emotional and mental level has not been achieved. A lack of this connection will ultimately lead to loss of interest and a breakup at best, and at worst it will lead to infidelity.

It's not difficult to comprehend the reasons why men find it next to impossible to take it slow, especially when we're talking about new relationships. Nowadays, most men who enter a relationship don't have any intention of connecting with the other person on an emotional level. Instead, they focus only on the physical connection. If you don't behave this way, you are associated with a "wuss".

There is a sort of peer pressure in many circles among men to "seal the deal" as soon as possible, as I'm sure you're aware. As I've said, this can set you up for a whole lot of disappointment because, if I may be so crass, most women with whom you can establish a valuable relationship will not be "easy." If you find a woman that's worthwhile and rush things and put pressure on her, you are likely to push her away.

Typically, falling "head-over-heels" in love with a woman imminently implies having sexual intercourse as soon as possible. And, this rush, which seems to be attractive and really intriguing at the moment, will lead to hasty decisions such as moving in together before you're actually ready to take this step. However, the worst part about these types of rushed decisions is that they lead to unfortunate breakups. Such events leave both partners dealing with emotional trouble and luggage.

But real men aren't looking for a relationship that's only based on sex. On the contrary, real men want to connect with their partners on a deeper level and attain a unique bond. Such men are confident and aren't afraid to court the women they appreciate. Contrary to popular belief, taking it slow doesn't mean that you're any less of a man than your other friends are, but, in fact, makes you a better man.

It displays that you are confident and that you respect yourself and the woman you are dating. It shouldn't come as an offense, while this may come into the discussion, taking into consideration the social implications that influence our relationships. However, the truth is that real men are keen on developing their intelligence and skills, carrying interesting conversations, and getting into sentimental depths with a woman, not into her bed.

Being a gentleman doesn't come without any hardship, that's for sure, and patience definitely proves difficult for many. It is important to foster such qualities, though, even if you don't find much approval and understanding around you. It's important because when a gentleman is out to attract a woman, he aims for quality over quantity. What does this mean in terms of attraction and relationships? It simply means that you don't want to attract just anybody, but a specific kind of person who's worth the effort.

The higher your standards are when it comes to both your own conduct and choosing a partner for yourself, the more difficult it may prove to establish a relationship with most people. The sad truth is that shallowness and a lack of values are hardly exclusive to men in this day and age. So, if you're having trouble finding a partner due to being gentlemanly, you should know that this is not a bad thing. The relationships that a gentleman gets into, although they may be rarer, are much stronger and more meaningful than what you would get by acting like everybody else.

This is what higher standards lead to. They require patience and passing on certain opportunities, but the long-term results make it all worthwhile because the relationship you can establish with a good woman by being a gentleman is worth a whole lot more than a thousand flings you can have otherwise. And seeing as you're reading a book about being a gentleman, I am willing to bet that you are looking for the former. Besides, building a lot into a relationship is quite eventful and fun actually, and it even gives you an actual purpose.

Please take a moment to read and analyze the quote I included at the beginning of the chapter. Do you get where I'm headed? A real man will savor every step of the road towards attaining personal intimacy with a woman, and he will enjoy every little stage as the relationship slightly develops. The anticipation and slow-paced rhythm will make your relationship much more intriguing and satisfactory; that's a given! Every woman deserves being truly respected and if your only association with a woman is physical intercourse, then, my friend, you are on the wrong path and need to change your mind.

You can make a woman feel appreciated and loved before you reach that phase in a relationship; I can assure you! Leave her breathless with a beautiful, romantic gesture she will highly value; aim at making her feel truly loved – kiss her hand, walk her home, carry her groceries, in simpler words, take care of her and show her in an apparent, straightforward manner that she is important to you.

If all the relationships you had before didn't have any deeper meaning, and you never truly connected with a woman, I have to say that you don't know what you have been missing. You need to comprehend that a relationship is so much more than what the media is trying to convey, and if you open yourself, she will too, and you'll reach a level of relationship maturity you never thought you would.

Not only are some of the ideas floating out there promoting general shallowness but they even go as far as to equate the whole concept of love with just sex. They may not state it directly, but many of the influential voices in the media make the whole thing revolve around it. If you're looking for a real life partner in a woman you want to be with, then you will have to be a friend as much as a lover.

The problem with impatience and anxiety to move things along fast goes well beyond just dating and the sexual aspect of relationships. Just look at the divorce rates in the developed world today, they are incredibly high. Of course, there is a multitude of factors that contribute to so many marriages falling apart, but haste and focus on the wrong things are certainly among those factors. People neglect the importance of establishing a firm and deep relationship that revolves around understanding and truly knowing the partner. The resulting commitment is thus doomed to fail, especially when challenged by the many other hardships of life that come into play later on.

A relationship is not a race, nor a quick subway drive, but a long, exciting and spectacular journey you and your dear one take together. If you let it follow its own pace, you will be amazed of the multiple surprises it has in range for you.

Chapter 5: L for Literacy

"A man's bookcase will tell you everything you'll ever need to know about him." - Walter Mosley

It is said that a true gentleman is the one who reads, and this is something I couldn't agree more with. Intelligence is definitely one of the most attractive character traits in a man. This subject is certainly a broad one, but it's no secret that every self-respected gentleman is well-prepared and aims at continually improving himself and his knowledge of the world.

When I'm referring to literacy, I'm not thinking of the way you were educated, whether you come from an educated and wealthy family or not. Certainly not. Instead, I'm talking about the intelligence that can be cultivated through the cultural habits you develop in your spare time. For instance, the books and newspapers that occupy your time, the gallery arts you choose to visit, the theatrical plays that seem appealing to you – all these, in a way, portray your character and speak thousands of yourself.

Intelligence, knowledge, and being well-read form one important aspect of a gentleman that isn't inborn or inherited. Nowhere is it clearer that a gentleman is a frame of mind that can be attained by anybody than in this aspect of personality. This doesn't depend on your material situation or family background whatsoever – it is wholly an effort that you consciously make.

We now live in an age of fast food, fast entertainment, communication, and fast relationships. Such a social setting has made the attention span of many people severely shrink over the past couple of decades. More and more people have real trouble with staying focused long enough to read a whole work of literature, let alone gain deeper knowledge and insight into the world or life itself. This lack of interest makes it increasingly difficult for young gentlemen to read on a regular basis and become more erudite. It is interesting and somewhat paradoxical, however, that this also happens to be an era where access to information and knowledge is easier and more available than ever before, especially thanks to the internet.

It is, therefore, merely a thing of your own choice and interest to start reading more and acquire wisdom. You may think reading is old-fashioned, not trendy, and a lot of those around you may feel the same. But, I would like to remind you once again that being a gentleman is all about attracting the right kind of women instead of every single one of them. And believe me, if you are well-read and intelligent, you will attract the same kind of person from the ranks of women as well – and there are still a lot of such women out there.

It's also important to note that reading will greatly increase your vocabulary over time, making you better at keeping a conversation going and even bolstering your sense of humor – a crucial ingredient of attractiveness and charisma.

Possibly, the main two attractive qualities in a man are his conversing skills and sense of humor. These make you a stand-up guy to the girl of your dreams, and to the rest of the individuals you come in contact with. These qualities will also be endlessly valuable to you for making your relationship work in the long run!

A man's intelligence is a valuable trait that helps him make things happen for himself. A real man won't wait for things to alter miraculously overnight, but he will make his dreams come true, and develop the traits he needs for achieving that.

Having a debate or conversation about art, literature or history doesn't make you a wuss or anything like, contrary to what your friends might think, but it will make you stand out of the crowd, and will genuinely grow your chances in front of women.

And let's admit it; at the end of the day, the girl you like will decide to go on a date with you only if you prove to her that you are more than just a pretty face. You know what I mean? A woman will want to be with a man who can handle a debate on a challenging subject, who has knowledge on more subjects – not only sports and his favorite basketball team. Your intelligence and level of culture will always be displayed in your conversations, and this is something you cannot fake.

Wit and a sharp tongue will impress most women actually, not just a few special ones. Everybody knows that women like a charismatic man, and there are many cases where a strong charisma can even be as effective as to overshadow other shortcomings a man may have. Being knowledgeable plays an important role in having such charisma. Keep in mind that this isn't the early 20th century when women were only getting the right to vote and pursue higher education. Times have changed a great deal. Most women today are sophisticated, educated, and ambitious individuals with a lot of interests and principles.

A modern woman doesn't want a crude, stereotypical male who'll bring her a wolf pelt from his hunting trip and then chop wood for the fire. Of course, there are still a lot of traditionally masculine traits that are very attractive to women, which is the way it should be, but nowadays it's important to exercise your mind just as much as anything else. A real gentleman is very masculine in nature; there is no question about this, and it is very important to find a balance. The difference between a gentleman and a brute, however, is in intellect, composure, manners, and wisdom. Gentlemen are principled, and they are men with a code of conduct, but they are very much men. Remember how I discussed the difference between a real gentleman and your run-of-the-mill nice guy at the beginning of this book?

Of course, it goes without saying that you should work on developing your intellect primarily for your own sake, as this is one of the most foolproof ways to go through life in general.

And this doesn't matter only in your relationship with women, but also in the way in which you interact with other individuals. Let's say that you have just met a person, and you start talking about your favorite novel or author or ask a couple of intriguing, smart questions, and then, the odds are that that person is already hooked. You see, such a guy will have managed to make a positive first impression.

The truth is that regardless of the topic this man is talking about, he will portray his knowledge, and he will know how to keep you interested during a conversation. Did you ever meet a guy who is unable to talk about a topic apart from say, sports? I know I did. And such a guy isn't an attractive fellow if you were to ask me, or any woman for a change.

Even if such a man was to find a girl who really cares about sports, and happens to like her a lot, a single topic can only carry the interest for so long before it gets old. This is why a man must be versatile in all regards, especially knowledge. But more than just providing you with information, reading will help you garner wisdom concerning everything from being happy to the way you interact with others. Certain books will even teach you a thing or two about the mysterious realm that the female mind often is.

A man who reads and is well-educated will know how to treat women correctly, as well as the people surrounding him. Another character trait most intelligent guys have, which, if you ask me, is unparalleled, is a good sense of humor! You might ask, what does sense of humor got to do with intelligence? The answer is: a lot. As a matter of fact, scientists tell us that there is a strong connection between intelligence and sense of humor. Of course, you don't have to be a genius to come up with run-of-the-mill jokes. But an exquisite, more subtle sense of humor will always be a sign of pure intelligence. In this direction, the environment and the social background of a person will have a significant impact on the individual's humor.

Typically, it all comes down to the individual's capability to comprehend different types of jokes. For instance, a gentleman will prefer dry, sarcastic jokes, in comparison with slapstick comedy or jokes with gross or sexual connotations. And, in many cases, the jokes a person says can provide you with a complete insight into his point of views on stressing social issues. In this view, some of the best comedians display intelligence in their routine. How is that? Because their jokes portray the most common social aspects of the present through funny examples.

Cracking an adequate joke that fits perfectly into your current setting or conversational topic is also a sign of a quick mind. If your brain is quick to connect dots and explore different combinations and options as you engage someone in conversation, helping you construct a quality joke, then it becomes obvious why humor relates strongly to intelligence. Moreover, coming up with something funny based on what you hear at a given time also shows that you are present and paying attention to the conversation.

Of course, you shouldn't use your wit and humor to ridicule others, even if your joke is really amusing. There is a difference between showing people a good time, making them laugh and having malicious intent to hurt someone's feelings. Jokes at the expense of others should be primarily reserved for the circles of very close friends and family, and should be avoided when you are meeting new people. A harmless and charming remark in good humor may be acceptable if you are on a date, perhaps, but you should be very careful. And most importantly, if you are willing to put the joke on others, make sure you are prepared to take the same like a gentleman and not get defensive if someone jokes with you in return. There is nothing more uncomfortable than a person who loves making fun of others but flips out when they respond in kind.

Chapter 6: E for Empathy

"Empathy is really the opposite of spiritual meanness. It is the capacity to understand that every war is both won and lost. And that someone else's pain is as meaningful as your own."- Barbara Kingsolver

Another equally important topic is empathy. Each of the personality traits I have mentioned above goes down to nothing if you don't aim at developing this feature as well.

Have you read the quote I included above? Empathy will and can transform your life. It will have an enormous impact on every little aspect of your existence. I'm talking about your personal well-being, and your relationships as well. Unfortunately, the greater majority of people fail to comprehend the actual importance of developing empathy – as it can literally change your way of thinking, the way in which you perceive yourself and others.

Typically, empathy can be conveyed as a person's capability to recognize and comprehend other people's feelings and situations. In a nutshell, empathy is similar to filling in someone else's shoes.

While empathy is indeed something you can work on and develop, it's important to understand that it is an innate component of human nature in any mentally fit individual. However, just like it can be developed, it can also be suppressed over time, and it often is in modern society. Empathy is seen every day, though, in all manners of interaction between people. It can be seen in the small and mundane things such as simply understanding someone's point of view, but empathy is also what drives heroic acts of compassion between fellow human beings.

A gentleman is the man that steps up in times of need and helps the afflicted. This is the individual who drags people out of a burning car, simply because he is compelled to do so, not because he wants recognition. Of course, it's unlikely that you personally are going to happen upon such a scene, storm the beaches of Normandy with your comrades, or end up in any extreme situation like that. So, it's most important for you to understand how empathy works in the day-to-day and what it can help you achieve.

As we have already covered early on, it's a me-orientated culture for the most part. It is, therefore, no surprise that we as a society sometimes lack empathy. There was a time when compassion and an empathetic connection between people was a necessary tool of survival, but that time is long gone by all indicators. Nowadays a person is conditioned to put themselves and their goals above all else and to pursue their ambition even at the expense of others.

Overly zealous careerism, for example, is quite a widespread phenomenon in modern society and it truly comes to light in many of our workplaces. Being empathetic and considerate of your coworkers when there is a possibility of a promotion or another gain is considered as a hindrance to one's professional success. After all, the very nature of competition requires us to focus on the shortcomings and weaknesses of our counterparts, not their feelings, hopes, and goodness.

A competitive environment may be one of the most difficult ones for a real gentleman. Make no mistake, though, as competition is no excuse to act like anything less. Competing and trying to better one's opponents is hardly a foreign concept for a gentleman. If you start to think about it, you'll even realize that chivalrous conduct was actually an integral part of any competition in our civilization throughout history, thus birthing the concept of honor.

Your workplace is definitely an environment where you will be tested and tried; sometimes feeling as though you should compromise your principles in order to get ahead. You should always look for alternative ways of achieving your goals, ways that don't require you to step on your values or stab somebody in the back. All things considered, it's not that hard to stay a gentleman even in the corporate world. The key is to make sure your greed never outweighs your commitment to staying true to yourself.

Most of your coworkers and even bosses will love you for it, but exercise caution because there are some individuals who will perceive your ethics as a weakness. This breed will try to take advantage of you and use your dignity against you. Such machinations hardly work out, though, as a real gentleman is no fool.

Finally, try to be the guy people can depend on at work, and help out the ones who struggle instead of stepping over them. If you look at things from their perspective you'll see them for what they are – just people trying to do their best. If you really excel at your work, you should try and give guidance to others, as this will slowly but surely put you in a leadership role. This position of leadership may only concern your relationship with colleagues at first, but it may very well turn formal in the form of a promotion if the higher-ups notice you for it.

Most of the times, on an unconscious level, we think about the persons surrounding us in a negative way, without even realizing it. This can be conveyed through a type of prejudice – judging people without actually knowing their individual situation and everything related to them.

Empathy for a man is a feature that will help him see those around him as equals. This way, he will be able to look beyond himself and his own needs. I don't know how this concept appears to you, but please hear me out – I want to introduce you to the main reasons you, as a gentleman, should develop this trait.

Men are different from women – nothing new and debatable here. For this reason, in many cases, it seems rather hard, even impossible, for men to comprehend girls and be empathic towards their needs or emotions. And I'm not necessarily referring to minor issues, such as being empathic over a chipped nail after an expensive manicure. And it's no need for you to start making up excuses that you're not the sensitive type of guy, and you don't have a natural inclination towards encouraging or understanding other people's needs, especially those women who are almost impossible to comprehend! But, believe me, this is the main excuse of the greater majority of men out there who are self-absorbed and care about their needs and feelings only. The moment you admit to yourself that all this stuff is naturally emerging as lame excuses rooted in your egocentrism, you are on the right path.

Empathy can be seen as a skill, and it can be developed into your second nature. It's as simple as that – put yourself into someone else's shoes, and try to understand why they are where they are, and what had contributed to their present situation. Ask yourself this simple, yet difficult question – "what would I do in that position?"

It's easy to see how empathy comes into developing a healthy relationship. Even when that special someone in your life is being irrational and unpleasant towards you by no fault of your own, you need to try and be understanding. As a matter of fact, this is when you need to be empathetic the most. Many of us carry emotional residue from many experiences in life, especially events in our childhood years. If you know a person well enough, you will always be able to see their perspective and understand where they are coming from and what's causing their behavior.

This is how empathy plays its crucial part in successful communication between people, especially close ones. If your past relationships lacked understanding and proper conversation, then the problem may be in that you couldn't effectively see your partner's point of view. This is definitely something to fix in order to avoid emotional disasters in the future.

In the eyes of a woman, empathy is one of the most important qualities a man can have. But, making abstraction of this aspect, being empathic will help you become a better person, a less selfish, less narcissist and less self-absorbed individual.

In some situations, being empathic will mean trying to be nicer to your girlfriend because she had a bad day at work, or because she had a fight with her best friend, and so on and so forth. This also includes one of the main things that for us, guys, is next to impossible to grasp – the dreaded days that are typical to PMS. Instead of disappearing for a couple of days, in order to avoid a possible fight, try to comfort your lady, and give her a nice cup of tea or get her a box of delicious chocolates.

Unless you are involved with a particularly malicious and manipulative person who means you harm, those hard days are something you should stoically bear and do your best to endure while maintaining a positive attitude. No woman in her right mind is going to remain indifferent to her partner's efforts to make nice and indulge her, regardless of what her hormones may be doing to her at the time. If you're trying hard enough, she will too, I assure you. After all, your woman is your partner, that's different from children, for example, with whom ungratefulness is almost unavoidable and just a fact of life.

Caring for other people's needs and feelings doesn't make you any less of a man, but makes you one of the very best. Apart from showing a woman sincere respect and appreciation, empathy will help you be next to her when she needs you the most and is going through something you don't get at that time.

Empathy doesn't mean that you're letting aside your beliefs and principles. It only means that you are open-minded enough to accept that other people may feel differently than you, and may choose to act distinctively.

You need to develop your ability to listen to others, and actually pay attention to what they say. Normally, discussions on intricate topics can make us, in many cases, lose our temper. In such cases, we tend to overlook other people's opinions because we assume we hold the single truth to all issues in life. Such an attitude does not portray that you're confident; it only shows that you're a narcissist, and you don't wish to accept other people's ideas. In my point of view, such a man is narrow-minded, and this is not the attitude of a gentleman.

Next time you find yourself in such a situation, since they are kind of inevitable, you should try the following exercise. Aim at taking other people's opinions into consideration, listen to their part of the story and be open minded. Think of the speaker's motivation that lies behind his/her standpoint. Think of his/her life and experience, which are essential factors that contribute to his/her way of thinking. Such an attitude will help build a powerful connection between individuals.

Empathy actually means that you care about other people, and the person you show compassion towards will feel appreciated and valued. Can you think of the last time a person showed you empathy, and do you remember how it made you feel? It felt good, didn't it?

At the end of the day, the real gentleman will be empathic, gentle, kind, generous and attentive. Typically, empathy is more about being a real man, as opposed to appearing manly. It's about considering other people's opinions as important as yours, and showing endless respect towards the persons in your life. A true gentleman is a man every woman will look up to and feel happy she is lucky enough to have in her life.

Finally, I should mention that empathizing with yourself to a small degree does not necessarily equal narcissism. Don't get so hung up on the notion of being everyone's shoulder to lean on that you overlook when someone is blatantly using your good will. Always help those in real trouble, yes, even if you don't particularly like them, but don't go out of your way to be their instrument at all times. A small portion of individuals are just not worth the effort, and it's imperative that you learn to recognize when someone is clearly working to your detriment. You can even be as empathetic as to understand a bank robber and the circumstances that have led him to do his deed, but you wouldn't help him in his act, would you? Like with anything else in life, common sense goes a long way with empathy as well.

Chapter 7: Lessons on Chivalry

"Some say that the age of chivalry is past, that the sport of romance is dead. The age of chivalry is never past..." – Charles Kingsley

I want to establish that being a real gentleman is so much more than dressing accordingly. While dress code inevitably carries a lot of importance, as I already talked about this matter in the first chapters of the book, the key to becoming a better version of yourself is educating your mental state and behavior. It's not difficult to comprehend why I'm saying this, as, even though you were to be the best-dressed man in the room, and your attitude wouldn't portray that of a gentleman, it would be all for nothing.

Let's establish one primary thing. Chivalry is not old fashioned, and will never be. The exact measure that indicates a man's value is respect towards himself and towards others, which is portrayed through chivalry.

Appreciatively, our society has made substantial progress concerning gender equality. Thankfully, the days in which women were perceived as property and inferior to men are gone. But, with this main advantage came a crucial side effect, which has made chivalry quite a problematic aspect. Gender equality causes the greater majority of men to treat women as if they were men. Even though it is crystal clear that men and women are equals, that doesn't mean you should treat a woman the same as you would a man. While this aspect is quite debatable, taking into account the modern day context, the truth is that every woman, deep inside, wants to be truly respected and treated like a lady.

Besides still having a prominent place in our contemporary society, it's also important to understand that being a gentleman also knows no age. A chivalrous attitude is a desirable trait for all men and boys in any age group.

You can thus teach your young child from an early age that being a gentleman is important. Make sure he understands that girls are different and that he shouldn't treat them how he would treat the rest of the boys his age. It helps a great deal if he has a sister of similar age, whom he can learn to respect, protect, and help from early on. This will serve to shape his worldview and make him adopt the right attitude for later in life. You'd be surprised by how much of our character is built and predetermined in our early childhood.

Of course, another crucial stage of life is the teens. This is where a young man's personality begins to become more consolidated, and all that he has learned up to that point plays an important part in shaping the kind of man he turns into. For most boys, it's also the age of crushing after girls and starting to get involved in relationships. The interactions between men and women change rapidly through different stages of life, and the aspects of gentlemanly conduct do as well. Girls at different ages also expect different things from boys and men.

It's unlikely that a teenager will be able to take his girlfriend out to a fancy dinner or the like, so it's about the little things at this age. Showing small acts of affection and respect like holding doors for girls, giving them his jacket when it's cold, and other small gestures like those are what make a teenage boy stand out as a gentleman in the making. The attitude develops from there on if fostered, and the teenager will grow into a man who respects women all his life.

A real gentleman never ceases to be such, though, not even in old age. By that time, he will have long found his companion in life and will have learned all her quirks and beauties, marking him as an expert on making her happy. There isn't all that much learning left to do at that point either, particularly when it comes to being a gentleman. A man that has maintained a happy marriage and carried it on into his late years is a doctor in the field anyway. As you will notice with a lot of elderly men, they are always kind and pleasant towards women they come into contact with during their day, regardless of their age.

Seeing as you're reading a book on how to be a gentleman, I doubt you are quite at that point yet, so we'll look into some signs of chivalry. Now, let's see some of the main principles a gentlemen should live by.

Treat everyone with genuine respect

I want to outline that a gentleman isn't respectful only to the women he is interested in. On the contrary, a gentleman is an individual who is actually attentive to other men, elderly fellows, and children as well. If you wish to adopt the attitude of a gentleman as a means to get a woman to like you, this isn't right! Such an attitude isn't something you turn on and off as you please, this would make you a hypocrite, and that's the last thing you want.

This may not be the first thing to occur to you, but being a gentleman has quite an important place in the interactions among men as well. Obviously, it's not about catering to their needs per se, because it works a little differently in male circles.

Carrying yourself gentlemanly with other men means adhering to a few basic principles, most of which relate to sportsmanship, honor, camaraderie, and empathy. First and foremost, being a gentleman means not taking cheap shots at your opponents, in any setting or circumstances. If you are competing for a promotion, for instance, it wouldn't be very chivalrous to sabotage your competition and employ other dirty tactics to get ahead. A gentleman also doesn't kick a man while he's down, neither literally nor figuratively. If you have differences with someone, don't jump the opportunity to get revenge as soon as they fall on hard times and things don't go their way. Raveling in another's failure and taking advantage whenever an opportunity presents itself is very lowly and unbecoming of a gentleman.

Furthermore, I don't know if I even have to state something as obvious, but a gentleman will never, under any circumstances, bully someone and prey on the weaker. There is no world in which this behavior is excusable and anything but an offense against basic human dignity. As a matter of fact, not only will a gentleman never bully someone weaker than him, he will even stand up for those who fall victim to bullies. Another thing that follows up on bullying and mistreatment of the weak, which a gentleman doesn't do, is the abuse of power and position in general. Using a position of influence as a means for personal gain, or simply using it to exert power on others just for the sake of exerting power, is highly unethical and dishonorable, to say the least.

And last but definitely not least, a gentleman doesn't start a fight. However, yet another difference between a gentleman and a guy who is merely nice is that a gentleman won't run away from a confrontation either. Of course, he will avoid unnecessary conflict, especially a physical one, if he can, but he won't do so at all costs. A real gentleman will be the kind of guy who doesn't look for trouble and can defuse almost any situation, which is why gentlemen rarely get into fights, if ever. However, life can throw you into a situation where the only alternative to getting into a confrontation is to compromise your very dignity, which a gentleman will never do. As a particular popular song has to say on the subject, "A gentleman will walk but never run."

As you have learned so far, though, it's crucial to be chivalrous in simpler ways and with little things that can happen every day if you are to project yourself as a gentleman all the time, not just in critical situations. Now, I would like to start with the basics rules of chivalry.

The magic of "Thank you", "Please" and "Excuse me"

These basic, yet essential phrases are more than crucial in outlining your character and respect towards the people you get in contact with. I personally taught my children these key phrases, and every self-respected man (and woman) should use them when needed. The use of these phrases can go a long way in helping you deliver the right impression.

Using "thank you" indicates your genuine gratitude towards the person who has helped you in a way or another. Also, "please" is the magical phrase that proves you are attentive and considerate of other people. Of course, "excuse me" is an equally powerful word combo that has imperial power. Every time you accidentally get into someone on the street or at work, you shouldn't hesitate to say "excuse me". This also applies for the situations when you need to leave the room or the table, especially when you're on a date!

What you get in exchange for using these everyday phrases is also important. More often than not, a nice word or two will open many doors for you. Most people are likely to be disarmed by such an approach, especially if it's coupled with a sincere smile, and it will be more difficult for them to be rude towards an individual who treats them well. Counter workers, for example, and employees in any sort of administration that deals with a lot of people daily, are known for being some of the most frustrated individuals you can run into. If you approach them with a poor attitude, it will only make the interaction even more unpleasant. If you are well-mannered, on the other hand, they are likely to be nicer to you in return. Why get into unnecessary altercations that could potentially ruin your day when you can have a pleasant chat instead? Who knows, your manners and smile may even change someone's day for the better.

Don't wait to open doors

After reading this, you might say – why should I be opening doors, it's not like I'm an usher or something? But, believe it or not, holding the door open, to some women, is definitely an attractive quality. Still, bear in mind that while some women may convey this gesture as lovely, others may find it inappropriate. For this reason, always ask before opening the door for someone. Only ask "May I hold the door for you?" According to the answer you receive, you will know what to do next.

Give up your seat

Whenever you are traveling using public transport, always pay attention to elderly citizens, pregnant women or women in general. If the place is packed, and you see a person struggling to stay on their feet, I would recommend you take the attitude of a real gentleman and offer your seat. You don't have to act unnatural, only ask a simple question such as "can I offer you my seat?" Such a simple gesture will speak for your character, and it goes a long way ahead of you.

The same goes for people holding babies or having small children with them. A gentleman is nice to kids, and people generally hold those who are good to children in very high regard. I can hardly think of anything less gentlemanly than a guy sitting and staring out through the window while someone next to him is struggling with a kid or few on a crowded train or a bus.

Meeting and greeting

Typically, there is a particular way in which introductions should be carried out. It is genuinely helpful to every one of you reading this book to find out the proper way to do this. Bear in mind that one of the worst and most offending things you can do is forgetting to introduce a person while you have a conversation with another individual he/she is not acquainted with. This kind of incident shows a lack of respect and consideration. I admit it happened to me once to overlook such a fact, and I felt genuinely bad afterward. However, after this incident, I was increasingly more attentive to this particular detail, and it didn't happen again. Thus, hopefully, if you are careful enough, this won't happen to you too.

For instance, let's say that you are meeting a person that is older than you. In this situation, you don't want to create the wrong impression by saying something inappropriate such as "what's up?", right? In such cases, your best alternative is a simple "hello".

Believe me, introductions shouldn't be conveyed as tricky. There are some simple rules you should bear in mind. Just remember that a person who has a higher rank must have the second person introduced to him or her. Or, the person who has a lower status has to be presented first.

For instance, Clark is your friend, and because of his age, he is considered of lower status, in comparison with Mr. Abbot, who is a CEO in the company you work. This is one of the basic guidelines you should take into consideration. Younger people should be presented to older persons, citizens to politicians or prominent figures, and men to women. If it's difficult for you to remember this right now, you should know it will become easier with time.

When you are introduced to somebody, try to concentrate on that person's name, because it's genuinely rude to forget the name of the person you have just met, and that, sadly, happens all the time. Also, make sure your handshake is firm, not too mellow, but it shouldn't crash that person's bones either. You get the idea.

If you happen to forget the newly acquainted person's name, however, it's no cause to panic really. You can use clever tactics to get it from that person or someone else again. The approach you can use will depend on the circumstances under which you have met the person. However, if you don't see a way to get their name repeated without directly asking for it, then it's not the end of the world to just ask either. You can even make it charming and funny with the right attitude, as a gentleman can do with most things.

A gentleman's behavior towards women

While the tips enumerated above surely apply when it comes to a real gentleman's behavior towards women, numerous other suggestions are equally powerful. One magic principle you should abide by in all circumstances is to be attentive to the desires of women.

- **Hold the door**

I know I already mentioned this magical gesture before, but you should develop this instinct especially when it comes to women. While there are a couple of women that break apart from the majority and are not keen on being pampered in this way, the greater majority – more than 95 percent of them – love this kind of gestures.

For this reason, try to develop it until it becomes a reflex. Simply smile at her and open the door to the car, to the building, to the house, so on and so forth. She will gladly appreciate your effort, and will feel spoilt.

It's not just about the act of opening a door itself. Obviously, she is more than capable of doing this on her own, without your intervention. This is a gesture that shows you are taking note of someone's presence and existence, which most women love. Not only that, but you are putting your own time and what you are doing at second, while she takes priority for a fleeting moment in your life. This is where the power of this gesture lies, and it is registered unconsciously.

- **Help her**

A true gentleman will always aim at helping the woman he is with, whether we're talking about carrying the groceries, taking her coat, or a simple yet intimate gesture such as holding her hand while climbing the stairs. Always, always help her when she's struggling with something heavy. But remember, such gestures count for nothing if you brag as you do them. Act as naturally as possible and smile!

Such actions are courteous and, lucky for you, will allow the chance for physical contact. I know that when you get to know a woman, it might be pretty uncomfortable and awkward to hold her chair, but, in time, it will turn into reflex, and the lady in your life will feel appreciated. Developing these habits will surely make a difference in your relationship, I guarantee!

- **Wait for her**

If it takes a little bit more for her to get ready for your date, don't start complaining that you've been waiting for half an hour. Also, don't ask her why it take her so long to be ready. It's extremely rude and might even ruin your date. Keep in mind that she's making all this effort of getting ready for you.

Remember that patience is one of the marks of a gentleman? This means the little things too. And if a woman you are meeting happens to run a bit late, don't mention it to her, especially if she's a new acquaintance and you are only starting to see each other. Believe me, she is most likely going to apologize as soon as she shows up, which you should accept and shrug off with a smile. Besides, it's not like you can't hold your composure for an extra fifteen minutes if you are actually excited about seeing her. You already went on a date, so you're most likely in no rush. Besides, throwing a remark her way for being late can also project insecurity. If she sees that her being late really got to you, then you may give off the impression that you were anxious about her not showing up at all. You don't want her to think this, as you want to come across as confident.

The importance of first impressions – what she sees on a first date

A friend of mine, Laura, decided to go on a date with a guy she met through a common friend. The following day, she said that even though the date went smoothly, her overall impression of him was not a good one, as he arrived 20 minutes late, and he didn't even bother to come up with an apology or reason for being late. You see, my friend, things like these matter A LOT. First impressions, especially when it comes to women, are more than important in establishing a strong connection.

Because you see, women are very attentive to everything, and when I say everything, I'm not exaggerating. She will notice even the tiny details about your behavior or personality; she will see how you styled your hair, and whether you put any effort in dressing nicely or not. And something like arriving late on a date will portray lack of interest and respect.

Dressing sloppily also shows that you don't care all that much, either about her or the date. Casual is fine, however, as you don't have to be flashy or overdressed. Don't forget that you can overdo your appearance as well and leave her with an impression that you are trying too hard or are obsessed with your own look. Going with something more neutral and moderate concerning clothes can also help your personality come to the forefront if you aim to harness your charisma.

To tip or not to tip – this is the question

Now, I would like to focus on another issue that probably raises a couple of question marks – tipping. And the answer to this rather controversial question is affirmative – a gentleman always tips.

You shouldn't convey the idea of tipping as a means through which you reflect your wealth if that's what you were thinking before. But tipping, typically, is the natural thing to do, especially when the service you received was a great one. To begin with, if you weren't aware of it before, the people who work in this type of positions depend on tipping to some extent. Perhaps some of you who are reading this book work in these domains as well and understand what I'm talking about. And even if you aren't part of this category, the decent thing for you to do is to tip when the situation requires so.

But, remember, you should always be subtle and discrete when you tip. If you are taking care of the bill on a date with a woman you're seeing, make absolutely sure that your tipping goes to the sidelines. It has to be a thing that "just happens" without any announcement or discussion. As a matter of fact, there will be no harm done if she doesn't see you tip at all. Remember, it's about showing gratitude for the service you just received, to the person who provided it, not about you flashing your cash. Also, I would like to outline that the situations in which you shouldn't tip are the ones in which the service was genuinely horrible so that you have to discuss with the manager. But, if you were offered great service, then, tipping is more than necessary.

I want to tell you that statements such as "I can't afford to leave a tip for every service" or "I'm not the one guilty for the fact that the greater majority of services require tipping" are unnecessary and immature. Such services have been around forever, and won't cease to exist in the foreseeable future, so, we, as gentlemen need to adapt and do our best to show our appreciation towards the people who offer us services.

If you are a generous tipper, you will make yourself a positive reputation, and will always receive excellent service. For instance, if you go to the same restaurants on a regular basis, the staff there will know that you like tipping and will always make you feel welcome. While this shouldn't be your primary concern, it comes as a perk.

Now, I want to tell you something that will convince you of the real necessity of tipping. A great variety of service workers doesn't receive an hourly wage. In many cases, they receive a

$3.00 per hour base pay, and this makes them depend on the tips they get almost. For this reason, if you don't tip, they are making less than the minimum wage. Now, do you understand why tipping is required on your behalf, as a gentleman?

Of course, it's true that it isn't your fault that the system is set up this way, but unless you're going to start a revolution you should at least help out with a tip in accordance with your means. It's the empathetic and compassionate thing to do.

Chapter 8: The Importance of Displaying Positive Body Language

"The body never lies." – Martha Graham

Whether you're speaking or not, your body language will always mirror what you're thinking and how you're feeling. This type of language will either portray confidence – one of the primary personality traits of a gentleman – or insecurity, the exact opposite. Of course that you want to present yourself in a positive light, don't you?

Before we look deeper into body language, a couple of things should be noted about insecurity in general. Insecurity and various forms of anxiety are becoming increasingly widespread in our society. This primarily stems from a fear of leaving a poor impression or embarrassing yourself in front of somebody else. A good way to alleviate insecurity is to stop analyzing every single move you make and every word you say. Instead, try focusing on the person you are talking to. Ask them questions and take the lead in the conversation. This way, you will leave them with doing most of the talking, which can be good in two main ways.

Firstly, you are giving them the floor and being a good listener. As you have learned through this book, this is something that can almost never fail with women and is a desirable trait of a gentleman in itself. Secondly, by asking questions and listening to your partner in conversation, you are being given information to process, which will occupy your mind and help you stop thinking about any insecurity you might have.

When you have something to focus on, your mind will become more centered, and you will attain better composure, both mental and physical. Otherwise, insecurity will be reflected by everything from your eyes to your whole body.

Are you aware that when you keep your hands in your pocket and your shoulders hunched, you are unconsciously reflecting that you're insecure, and you're not willing to interact? Ask yourself the following question – how do you perceive a man who keeps his arms folded when in public, or even worse, when he talks to you? What is your first reaction towards the person who gives you a wet, trembling handshake? Or how do you act in the presence of a man who regularly bites his fingers or takes his hand through his hair?

I believe you get the hint. Now, if you are one of the men who displays this sort of body language, I would like to give you a couple of tips on how to surpass them, and develop your confidence. A gentleman has to indicate that he respects himself, and is confident. You have to get a clear impression concerning self-trust. Confidence does not equal pride, but it shows that you respect yourself, and those around you. Now, which are the main aspects when it comes to non-verbal communication, and how can you develop a positive body language? Here are a couple of basic tips.

Eye contact

How often did it occur to you to carry a conversation with a person that is unable to look you in the eyes? Possibly, he gazed at you for a couple of seconds during the entire duration of the conversation, but, soon afterward, his eyes castaway towards the ceiling or his shoes. Unfortunately, the greater majority of men are struggling with this particular aspect. Women seem to be better at the whole eye contact equation when compared to men. Don't ask me why, but it's just the way it is – they seem to be more confident when compared to us.

But why is it so hard to make eye contact for the greater majority of us? In most of the cases, we tend to hesitate to make eye contact because we are either masking our emotions or feel insecure about our status, knowledge or personal background. Typically, negative feelings such as anger, despair and disappointment are deeply hidden in our eyes. And, if those who experience these emotions want to protect themselves, they will avoid making eye contact.

Plus, eye contact imminently implies social interaction. People who are insecure want to avoid interaction at all costs, and will steer clear of making eye contact. But what is the root of these insecurity related issues? Typically, people who have a higher status are bound to make more eye contact when interacting with others. Meanwhile, the ones who have a lower status will avoid eye contact. Most of the times, a guy will do this because he doesn't feel that he is equal to the person he is interacting with. As mentioned before, this shortage of confidence can be linked to insecurity related to a person's appearance, the state of mind, culture, background, so on and so forth. It depends on every person.

If you find yourself in one of the situations mentioned above, you needn't despair. However, in spite of the fact that it doesn't come naturally to you to make eye contact with the person you are talking to, that doesn't mean you shouldn't work on it. Everything can be fixed with willpower and self-discipline, even your body language. The actual foundation when it comes to the ability to make eye contact comes from deep within. As you alter your way of thinking and living, you will feel better about yourself, surpass your insecurities and it will come naturally to look at people while smiling.

Eye contact indicates that you are confident, emotionally stable, competent, honest and attractive. You may ask, what does eye contact have to do with attractiveness? A lot, my friend.

First, eye contact constructs an intimate bond. It can design unique, yet memorable moments that allow you to get an authentic glimpse into someone else's feelings. Plus, confidence is, to some extent, connected to attractiveness. And as eye contact makes you appear secure, it will also make you more appealing – not only to women but to other people as well.

I acknowledge that, at first, this might be quite uncomfortable and pretty awkward to you, especially if you didn't focus on this until know. But, as you aim at developing this skill, it will become second nature, that's a given. For instance, try looking yourself in the mirror, and afterward, practice it in the presence of your family and close ones, and it will become easier to do the same with your co-workers and lady friends.

Your posture

Your position is crucial in displaying your attitude and feelings. It is, possibly, one of the essential things concerning nonverbal communication, which has a substantial impact on the way in which others perceive you. In simpler terms, nonverbal communication, in some cases, reveals more than verbal communication about a person. A lowered shoulder posture is typically linked to insecurity and lack of confidence. Crossed arms or legs can signal a feeling of closeness, detachment, and even hostility.

Meanwhile, a straight up posture will indicate that you are confident. The position will also determine an individual's degree of involvement in a conversation, as well as his attention.

An open posture will display positivity and friendliness. According to studies, the individual who adopts an open position is more persuasive and creates a good first impression. If you take this posture, and combine it with a relaxed facial expression, as well as positive eye contact, you are on the right path, my friend.

Our postures are mostly based on our primal nature. If you look into it, you'll find that body language is present with animals as well. All species, including our own, have a set of body language signals that serve to ward off predators, attract a mate, socialize, etc. They will thus clearly display feelings such as attraction or fright to those who know how to read them. Those aspects of our behavior that stem from natural impulses are the ones that a gentleman pays particularly close attention to. If you take a step back and really look at the whole picture, you'll see that being a gentleman is, at the most fundamental level, all about controlling one's primal nature. A gentleman thus moves himself as far away from the animalistic side that we all have, and closer to something higher that makes us different from animals.

If you learn to read the body language of others properly, you will find this ability to be very useful as well. Women, for instance, are all about body language as well. More often than not, you will be able to discern whether a woman likes you or not based on her body language. If she is attracted to you, she will strive to establish any form of physical contact with you, whether it's to touch your shoulder, face or hand. Even if it appears completely nonchalant, it almost always means something. She will also frequently touch or adjust her hair in your company and establish as much eye contact as possible.

Gestures

Our gestures become second nature and fostering various gestures such as pinching your fingers, touching your face or grabbing your ear, will only indicate that you are either nervous or not present in a conversation. I suggest that you analyze your behavior, especially when in public, and try to control your natural inclinations towards similar gestures.

Another thing that a lot of nervous people do is to tap their foot, displaying a so-called restless leg. This often becomes a habit that you may not even notice, but other people definitely will. The first thing that occurs to people when they observe somebody doing this is that the person is very nervous and uneasy.

Say cheese

An honest, open smile can go a long way, trust me. Regardless of your occupation or your personality type, choosing to smile can genuinely improve your look and change the way in which those around you convey you. Is this for real? Yes, it is. And as a bonus, women love men who smile. And as long as you are attentive to your dental hygiene, there's no reason you shouldn't use your smile to your advantage.

An honest smile will always reflect confidence and a positive attitude, which are both equally attractive qualities. A smile will indicate that you are an open person. If you start smiling more, you will realize that more and more people will begin smiling back at you, and that feels incredibly good!

On the other hand, a smile that is obviously fake or forced will do you no good. In fact, it can put most people off and make you very unattractive. It's better to smile rarely but sincerely than to go around with a grin that's just for show. This too can become habitual for some people, as I'm sure you have noticed. Having an artificial smile is particularly common for people in certain professions that require them to do this, making them seem very robotic and unpleasant. Sincerity is one of the most important traits a gentleman should have, and nothing reflects sincerity of character better than a smile.

The handshake

One of the things that count most in non-verbal communication is steering clear of a fish-dead handshake, which is weak and proves insecurity. If you want to kill all your chances at a successful interview, the one thing you have to do is give a weak handshake. On the other hand, though, it is also important that you don't crush the person's hand as you shake his/her hand. Also, the last tip concerning your handshake is to keep it simple, and by that I mean you should avoid opting for some elaborate teenage-like moves, which will indicate that you are immature and will create an awkward situation.

Chapter 9: Maintaining a Healthy Mental Outlook

Experiencing depression from time to time is normal. Life is a like a rollercoaster, with its ups and downs and it's only normal that it's this way. But every time something negative happens, we tend to feel under the weather and leave the negativity to overwhelm us. In many cases, the root of all evils such as alcoholism and drug use lies in depression. And there's no reason you should leave negativity rule over your life because you'll have so much to lose in this situation.

The key to steering clear of depression and its adverse outcomes is developing a positive mindset, and trying to maintain a healthy mental outlook. The truth is that every one of us has the potential to do something great about himself, but many of us fail to do that because we don't believe in ourselves.

As you have probably gathered by now, a gentleman is someone who definitely doesn't lack faith in himself and his abilities. Above all else, he knows himself for all his virtues and flaws, and he is thus in control over his emotions and thoughts, which ultimately results in having control over his own life as well. It's important to understand that the way your life is relates closely to the kinds of thoughts that spin around your head.

Even when things don't go well and life throws a curveball, a confident and focused man will not let the circumstances get to him, and he will never lose sight of his end goal. This is why it's important to adopt a certain perspective when it comes to pursuing a big goal in life. That perspective is the one where you don't let small obstacles and setbacks make you stumble and lose track. Each time you run into a snag along the way, no matter how difficult it may be, just keep your crosshairs on what you are truly after. Stay focused, and you'll find that life offers many alternative paths towards any end.

Taking your journey one day and one step at a time is not a bad strategy, though. It's not good to go to the other extreme where you focus on nothing but the goal and ignore what's right ahead of you. A man who is committed to success will set smaller and more proximate goals that each take him a step closer to the main objective every time he achieves a small triumph. But then again, you shouldn't make the mistake of becoming preoccupied with small things and actions to an extent where you lose sight and become lost yourself, forgetting where you were going in the first place or losing ambition.

In a nutshell, it's all about taking the punches as well as you can while always looking to the horizon at the same time, reminding yourself of why you sacrifice, fight, and persevere. Add to that a positive, optimistic attitude and there's only more power to you.

In this chapter, I would like to tell you how important it is for you to be positive, and how to control your outlook on life.

Happiness is a matter of choice

You read that just right. It all comes down to this single phrase – happiness is a question of choice. Life comes with the possibility to make decisions. Every time we wake up in the morning, we can choose between being positive or negative, and believe it or not, this little detail can make a world of a difference in the long run. You can test it for yourself.

Each day comes with a challenge. You need to accept this and aim at facing these challenges the best you can. All of us go through experiences in life that make us feel discouraged, but, with the right attitude, everything can be better.

The moment you allow the events in your life to dictate your mood, then, my friend you will become a slave of mood swings. I bet that you don't want to become the slave of your feelings, am I right? When you become a slave, you imminently lose your liberty. For this reason, you cannot cave into your impulses of behaving in a certain way, only because you feel that you have been poorly treated, or something unfair happened to you. On the contrary, the moment you choose to set yourself apart from all this, in a way, you are making a positive choice towards attracting happiness in your life.

But allow me to ask you something. What is happiness to you? How do you perceive happiness and what do you associate it with?

Now, let me provide you with my definition of happiness. First and foremost, we can say that happiness is reflected in your inner peace and satisfaction directed towards your life. Typically, we feel happy when there are no negative sentiments to make us feel bad about ourselves. While joy may seem like an immediate outcome of the external events that occur to us, in most of the cases, it comes from the inside and has nothing to do with external happenings. The truth is that happiness is a matter of choice and self-control.

Why does bliss seem to appear as an impossible target to the greater majority of people? Do you recognize that you are part of this category? Why does this happen? Because these individuals leave the external events in their lives take over and shadow their happiness. But, one of the keys to attaining happiness is embracing reality and achieving inner peace by developing positive thinking. It's genuinely important because, the moment you become in control of your own life, happiness will become a habit.

You may wonder what "embracing reality" truly means as pertaining to your own life. Well, it's certainly not about coming to terms with things that you can change and giving up on your goals just because you recently were struck by a setback and your plans have gone awry. Embracing reality means understanding a very simple truth of life – you can't control everything. As a matter of fact, you can't even control most things. There is always going to be some unforeseen turn of events with which life can surprise you, and sometimes this can derail a whole line of plans you've been building. A stable and confident individual will roll with the punches when they come and will improvise to surmount any hurdle he may encounter. So, the trick is to realize that a lot of what happens is beyond you and that this is okay. Take hardship as a challenge through which you can prove your worth, don't let it get you down and change your outlook on life. Instead, turn to yourself, as that is where the root of all happiness and sadness is.

What better evidence is there that our mood and attitude are influenced by something within us than those of us who are perpetually sad and miserable? Think of it this way. Good things happen to everyone who has at least a somewhat normal life. In fact, pleasant experiences can even happen to a person who is out on the street, with no roof or shelter over their head, let alone someone who has a house, a job, or even a family. And yet, you can see that a lot of people who have these things and much more in their lives are miserable nonetheless. This clearly goes to show you that the source of their dissatisfaction with life lies within and dictates that they have a poor mood regardless of outside circumstances. Some people feel so low, in fact, that they can't even enjoy the good things that happen anymore. This is a truly sad and painful state to be in, and what makes it even sadder is that the solution is up to the individual who is suffering.

Another thing that is very important if you are to maintain a positive attitude is not to look for someone or something else to blame for your misfortune. People often look to outside factors when things don't go as planned. This keeps an individual stuck in place because they refuse to address the real issues and are just searching for excuses to fail on an unconscious level. If they feel like they can't achieve something or are afraid to take on life, they will point the finger at someone or something outside that is supposedly precluding them from living up to their potential. This serves only to make one more comfortable in failure, and it's a lie most of the time.

If things don't go your way, it's either because the task you set for yourself was too difficult and unrealistic at the time and it ends up being one of those things beyond your control, or you have made a mistake or miscalculation. A real gentleman will always see when he has made a mistake, and he will own up to it and do better. If the former strikes, though, he will manage the situation as well as he can and just try again next time.

And finally, yet another majestic mental trick that can do wonders for improving your outlook is perspective. A whole lot of bad things can happen to us in life; there is no question about it; a tough breakup, getting laid off from work, debt, and loss. But always remember that a huge number of people out there have it infinitely worse. While you may find yourself all torn up over a relationship that just ended, ready to turn to the bottle even, someone, somewhere is on their deathbed, terminally ill, physically disabled, or even bleeding to death in the street.

Perspective isn't about finding solace in another's pain and misery, though, nor is it about exposing your mind to horrible tragedies around the world; it is about humbling yourself before life and tackling your problems like a man. Personally, I have always found that putting things in perspective helps a great deal. If I am struggling with something and then I consider the horrifying situations many others face, I quite honestly begin to feel ashamed to complain. Instead, I become motivated to cherish what I have and make the most of what I am blessed with.

Useful tips on how to stay positive

- Try to concentrate on the positive side of each situation. This will help you convey every situation differently, and will assist you in eliminating negativity from your life. A little humor goes a really long way in this regard too! Believe me, some people can find the joke in any situation that you can imagine, quite literally. This may be just my subjective impression, but it always seemed like those people who live under tougher circumstances and are used to hardship have the most lively and developed sense of humor. Good humor is really the cure for our souls, and it can mend a whole lot of pain in life.

- Try to concentrate on finding solutions to your problems instead of focusing on the problem itself.

- Develop relaxing habits such as listening to calm, soothing music that appeals to your taste. Various practices such as meditation, exercise or writing in a diary are also very helpful in this direction.

- Save at least half an hour every day for reading. That is a practical exercise for your mind, being equally relaxing as well.

- Aim at controlling your thoughts; the moment you notice that negativity gets over your mindset, focus on the positive side instead.

- Save some time every day to do something you love – whether we're talking about a book, a walk, a movie, or dinner, don't neglect yourself. The things that seem unimportant and insignificant can genuinely make a difference.

- Try to make other people happy as well by making simple, generous compliments or appreciative remarks. The moment you make someone feel better about themselves, you will become more content with yourself.

- Don't compare yourself with other people – most of the times, we are unaware of everything other people go through, and we have a subjective approach to their lives, and this might make us believe something that is untrue.

- Try smiling more often, and be nicer to the people surrounding you.

I hope that these tips are helpful to you my friend, as they are to me daily. Try to include these tips into your routine, and, one step at a time, you will begin to feel better about yourself and your existence. Remember, it's all about controlling your emotions and directing your attention towards the good things in your life, instead of the bad ones. And trust me, such an attitude is highly attractive to women. No woman wants to be with a whiny guy who does nothing but complain about everything bad happening to him. Plus, positivity will help you accomplish your professional goals as well, giving you confidence and reassurance.

Do's and Don'ts

Do's

- Comprehending that the life of a gentleman is, first and foremost, a matter of personal choice and every individual can turn it into a lifestyle, regardless of his personal background and occupation. As a matter of fact, working towards educating and improving yourself despite the potentially difficult circumstances of birth and your environment is one sure sign of being a gentleman. The harder the road, the more impressive the arrival is. That means that self-improvement gains meaning and leaves a much more powerful impression if the gentleman in question has had the odds stacked against him, with many temptations and excuses to go astray.

- Understanding that shaping your character shouldn't interest you only because it will make you more attractive towards women, but because it will help you become the best version of yourself. It's about living life in a certain manner and not about an ego trip or about procuring some tool to use against others. At the end of the day, a gentleman conducts himself as such because he feels he should, and because it's a comfortable way of life for him. If he helps someone out, he does so purely for the purpose of helping that person. Being a gentleman is thus not a means to an end.

- Learning that a real gentleman won't boast his generosity or wealth by making irregular and flashy gestures, but will always manage to be subtle when the situation asks for it.

- Remembering that, even though women are equal to men, they still need to be treated differently from men, like ladies. That is the first step towards a better understanding of women and how you should fulfill their expectations.

- Determining that you need to set yourself apart from the majority in order to lead the life of a real gentleman. As long as you take into consideration the current points of views that commonly occur as a result of social media and other aspects, you won't be able to develop such a lifestyle.

- Being a good influence on others is also a part of a gentleman's description. He will not forcefully spread his ideas and values and try to indoctrinate others into his way of thinking, but he will inspire those who have the capacity to be better. A gentleman inspires others simply by being who he is, so he does it quietly and without any sort of preaching. It's not your mission, nor should it be, to spread the word and go around vocally pointing to everyone's errors of their ways. The impression a true gentleman leaves wherever he goes is more than enough to show others that they too can be a better version of themselves.

Don'ts

- You shouldn't think that if you aim at perfecting your skills when it comes to personal grooming and appearance, you will be able to stand like a gentleman, and you no longer need to shape your inner character traits. You can't afford to be an empty shell that only looks nice on the outside. Your appearance is there to open many doors for you, but once you start to speak, the kind of man you are comes to light instantly. A gentleman will impress with his slick look and standing, but he conquers and really shines once he begins to exhibit his fine inner qualities and manners.

- You shouldn't assume that once you begin implementing the changes I included in this book your life will become entirely different, and women will start noticing you and your professional life will flourish. The lifestyle of a gentleman is something that you develop over time, and it takes patience and determination on your behalf. What we said about patience and taking it slow doesn't only apply to interacting with women and getting into relationships. What's very important is that a man must sometimes be patient with himself. Some habits and attitudes are really hard to change, and it can get even more difficult in later stages of life, once someone's personality is firmly established. It's alright to take a slow approach to improving yourself, as long as it is a continuous effort.

- Stop comparing yourself to other people, as, in many cases, this can lead to many other insecurity problems. There are cases in which comparison can be positive, but, in most of the situations it is discouraging, so, try to avoid that. You never know all of the circumstances and experiences that another person has had along his way. There are always going to be some who are more successful – this is an irrefutable truth of life. But, comparing yourself with others usually serves absolutely no purpose but to make you feel worse about yourself. The tricky part is that many people have this mentality instilled into their minds by their parents in early childhood. Parents who constantly compare their kids to their peers are bound to cause insecurity in their child's character. If you have children, you should avoid doing this at all costs. Everyone has their redeeming qualities, and instead of focusing on what they don't have, they should strive to perfect what they are blessed with. As long as a person does their best with what they've got, and adheres to certain values, he is on a trajectory to success.

- Don't leave your past experiences shadow your self-confidence and deter you from leading the life of a gentleman. It is best for you to let your past teach you how to be a better man, instead of discouraging you from becoming the best version of yourself. Many of us carry a lot of baggage in life, especially emotional weight. Most of these things are etched deep in our minds and can't be forgotten. That's okay, though, as the point is not to forget your past anyway, it's about learning to live with it. Everything that has happened in your life is your experience and nobody else's; it is an integral part of who you are. Embracing your identity and being at peace with yourself is one of the best ways of developing confidence.

- Don't ever compromise what you have built into yourself for any sort of gain, financial or whatever kind. A real gentleman is unshakeable in his dedication to being the man he is. He will never go back on his word and what he believes is right. A gentleman also listens and pays heed to other points of view, though, so he is open towards having his mind changed if presented with a solid argument. But when it comes to the qualities that make him a gentleman, he will never surrender and step on himself.

- Don't assume that leaving the life of a gentleman requires a particular occupation or age. This guide applies to all men out there, and will bring you enormous personal and professional satisfactions; I assure you.

Conclusion

I would like to show my gratitude towards each of you who has purchased this book, and for putting the time aside to read it. I honestly believe that the information this book contains is helpful to you, irrespective of your personal background and occupation. This guide is an important breakthrough for the men who are aiming at improving their personal and professional life.

I know that you feel as if millions of thoughts are running through your head at the moment, and you might be a bit overwhelmed. However, it's crucial that you take everything you have just read and implement it into your everyday life one step at the time. Haste can be our biggest enemy in most cases, so take things slowly.

I believe that, through this book, you have managed to get acquainted with the steps you should take on the process of becoming a real gentleman, and the main reasons it should be one of your priorities. The good part is that you have succeeded in acknowledging that you need change, and this step is vital. In fact, this is the exact spot from where it all gets started.

I would also like to remind you that the information this book includes should become a lifestyle because a gentleman is more than meets the eye. Personally, I believe that whatever a gentleman puts his mind to do is viable to become reality. The good manners of a real gentleman represent one of the keys to professional and relationship success. This is crucially important, because, nowadays, real men have become naturally extinct, and being a gentleman will soon become a lost art.

However, as long as there are men like you out there, men who possess an interest in behaving like something much higher than the current standard, this art continues to stand. Each time someone at least tries to work on developing their character towards being more gentlemanly, this olden but golden way of life continues to be perpetuated.

When I see photographs of earlier times, I see gentlemen who are dressed appropriately. But now, as a sheer contrast, I see men who are more likely to look like boys who didn't surpass adolescence and I see men who don't know how to treat a woman with respect and appreciation. But we don't have to fit in this social pattern, we can aim at being different and living the lives of gentlemen who respect themselves and the women in their lives.

It's true that judging a book by its covers is not the best thing for us to do, but indeed, you can create a strong opinion on a person based on their appearance, manners, clothes, and actions. Evidently, you know the expression – your actions speak louder than your words. If you don't foster the values and principles we've covered since we began, and if you are still the same as the rest on the inside, nobody will care about your appearance for longer than fifteen minutes after meeting you. There are the colors you wear, and then there are your true colors. Needless to say, the latter is what leaves the most lasting expression and will decide whether you attract or turn away that special kind of people.

This book outlines that being a gentleman is more than being well-dressed and groomed. The life of a gentleman is reflected in your lifestyle. Allow me to introduce you to a Chinese proverb that says – "unless we change our direction, we are likely to end where we are headed." That leads me to the question – is your life headed towards the direction you intended? If not, why not change yourself and become a man who makes his own destiny? This book explicitly points that becoming a gentleman is a matter of choice, and each of you reading this book has it within himself to become a better man.

Keep in mind that you are the one who knows best what is wrong and what needs to be changed in the way you live your life and interact with people. This book offers universal guidance for men, but no book in the world can look to the depths of you and tailor itself to your personal experience. It's up to you to think hard and see how the general concepts of being a gentleman apply to your story, as well as where these concepts are most fitting for you. Contemplate the wisdom critically and embrace it wherever needed, but I am willing to bet that you are already quite a decent fellow anyhow.

For me, living as a gentleman has been genuinely helpful in many respects. To begin with, it has helped me to convey every aspect of life with more attention to detail. I confess that this particular issue has a beneficial impact on my relationships and in my personal life as well. The life of a gentleman allows you to embrace everything with increased attention, and by everything I'm referring to my own style, work principles and relationship guidelines. This book stands as a translucent example of how to act like a gentleman and how to be one. Once more, I would like to thank you for downloading this book, and, let's live this life as real gentlemen! Thank you for your endeavor.

THANK YOU!

If you liked this book, why not leave a review on Amazon? Being an independent publisher on the ever-growing eBook market, every review you post helps us reach more people and provides us with important feedback to better serve you and other readers in the future.

Also, don't forget to join the Lean Stone Book Club. It's the best way to stay up-to-date with all our books, activities and promotions. Furthermore, you'll get various opportunities to contribute to our book club (and even get rewarded for it).

>> http://leanstonebookclub.com/join/ <<

Thank you once again for reading our book! All our kudos go to you!

LEAN STONE BOOK CLUB